The 24 Hour Society

To my father
and the memory of my mother

Contents

Foreword

An early draft of this book arrived on my screen at a hotel in Tempe, Arizona, early one Saturday morning in November 1998. I read the contents, on and off (as time permitted) that day, evening, and the next day on a flight to Los Angeles. As I type this it is mid-afternoon the next day, Sunday, and I am beside a swimming pool at a hotel in Santa Monica, California. Next to me is a bottle of Evian Natural Spring water from France, the *Sunday Times* from England, and a bag of savoury biscuits from Belgium. Because of my travel and work schedule I have to satisfy this request for a foreword today. Only five years ago this would have been impossible, but now, for me and many like me, it is the norm. We have become both customer and supplier, and technomads, on a shrinking planet where there is no escape, and where we choose to work when and where we wish.

If there was a twenty-first century bible of marketing and sales the opening paragraph would undoubtedly start:

> Customers don't want choice, they want what they want, when and where they want, and at a price and quality they dictate.

And how different this is from the twentieth-century version, which comes from a more sedate industrial, technological and social era, and starts:

> Customers want choice, our choice, supplied at a place and time of our choosing, at a price and quality we dictate.

What is happening to promote such rapid and radical change? In short, a transition from a world dominated by atoms to a world dominated by bits. If you live in a village you have to do everything, there is little supplier and customer choice, and the economy is bounded. But if you live in a city, you can afford to specialize, and you get a vast supplier and customer choice linked to a vast economy. IT and telecommunications are transforming our world into a global city with people and intelligent things (machines, sensors, actuators, photocopiers, food dispensers and complete production plants) communicating over networks of optical fibre, copper, radio and satellites. The bit economy is with us, and with it comes increased competition, availability and the disintermediation of markets.

If you want money on a Saturday at 9.30 p.m. where do you go? Not to the bank, but to the cashpoint at the supermarket. You want to order a book on a Wednesday at 8 p.m., where do you go? Not to a bookshop, but on-line to Amazon. Do you need the hassle of organizing travel insurance for every trip? No! Just use Master Card or American Express and it comes with the ticket purchase.

People in the USA have enjoyed 24 hour shopping since the mid-1980s; Europe is only just waking up to the prospect and the UK is leading the way. While Europe worries about the Information Society, how to limit working hours and how to control bits, the Americans are creating an Information Economy that is free and unbounded. This is where the future lies, and it is why Europe will see its 'lunch eaten' by competition rising to the challenge of the 24 Hour Society.

At the time of writing, my parent company, British Telecom, has over two hundred companies inside the group, and over sixty joint ventures on the boil. The vast majority of these are outside the UK and the same time zone. We have become a global entity, a wired and often virtual corporation with vast numbers of people working to maintain and expand a 24 hour, 365 day a year, spatially unlimited business far beyond the shores and thinking of the UK and mainland Europe. For me as an individual, this means responding to email within twelve hours, every day of the year, irrespective of where I am or what I am doing. It means I have to be able to communicate and work from any location and any time in order to respond to my customers the instant they call – for I am in a fiercely competitive global market. For my staff it means working unusual and unscheduled hours to appear, in reality or virtually, anywhere on the planet.

Now as a customer what do I and my staff expect? Pizza and coffee at 4.30 a.m. any day of the week. New clothes and electronic hardware purchases at 10 p.m. on a Saturday night. Why not? And it is not just us – it is an increasing percentage of the working population. IT is creating a new two-class society:

- Class 1: those who spend a lot of time trying to save money
- Class 2: those who spend a lot of money trying to save time

Stone Age Man worked only an estimated fifteen hours a week. In this new economy most of us will be working fifteen hours a day doing things that are far less risky than hunting for meat on the hoof, but sometimes, equally stressful. We need a 24 Hour Society to survive.

So what of this book? At last someone has taken a more holistic view and presented reasoned arguments, facts and figures, fears, hopes and encouragement for the future of our society as it changes faster than before. *The 24 Hour Society* covers everything from work, trading, sleep deprivation, zombie schedules, morning and evening people, circadian rhythms, transport, violence, morality, time management, ideologies, libraries, manipulating the biological clock, educational and other societal implications, regulation, archaic laws and much more. It is a fascinating and engaging book which will become an essential primer for those in government, commerce, education, healthcare, or just plain sitting in an armchair anticipating the future.

Peter Cochrane
BT Head of Research
Poolside
Miramar Sheraton Hotel
Santa Monica CA
November 1998

Acknowledgements

Many people have helped me formulate my views on the 24 Hour Society, without necessarily agreeing with them in any way. Others have helped in the making of this book, sometimes in ways in which they may not have even been aware. In particular I wish to thank Marc Dorfman, Dr Russell Foster, Marty Goldensohn, Dr Neil Goldman, Dr Keith Haarhof, Melanie Howard, Dr Mike Karger, Stuart Lansley, Nick Rand, Michael Willmott, James Woudhuysen and the officers in local authorities who were generous with both their time and comments.

All the faults in the book are mine alone. Any virtues, however, owe much to my editor, Nicky White, who has been tenacious in keeping me to the subject whenever I have tended to wander down indulgent and irrelevant byways. This book would not have come about without the publisher, Andrew Franklin, who acted on his wife Caroline's intuition and decided that this was a subject worth writing about.

Even well-organized people put pressure on their family when they write a book. I am not in that category, so I particularly wish to thank my wife Linda, for her encouragement and her tolerance of the ups and downs of writing, and my daughters Sophie and Leah for accepting the demands on my time.

Introduction

It may be so obvious as to be clichéd but the pace of change is increasing as our society is driven by fast-moving technological innovation. Cloned sheep, ears grown on the back of mice, water found on the moon, drugs for impotence, Fermat's theorem solved – we are living in a technological cornucopia that is moving and reshaping the earth under our feet.

The new technologies are having a dramatic effect on the small but vital details that make up our everyday lives. Holidays can be booked over the telephone and insurance bought around the clock. Car manufacturers allow customers to specify their own car and its options by touch screen or on-line imagery. Dixons, Tesco and Sainsbury among large retailers offer Internet services. Booksellers, bankers, florists, travel agents, manufacturers of domestic goods and clothing and many other sectors attract customers through electronic shopping 'malls'.

Bill Gates has, perhaps provocatively, called all this 'shoppers' heaven'. Over 50,000 companies in the UK advertise over the Internet to 4.6 million Internet users at home and in the office. Computers can be programmed to seek out a product at the best price world-wide, and even negotiate better deals with the computers of various sellers. By the year 2015 IBM estimates that 50 per cent of all retailing will be electronic, which could mean that thousands of jobs will be switched from the shop floor to call centres or Internet service companies.

All this electronic shopping can be done at any time, day or night, during the week or at the weekend. It is a key element of what is known as the 24 Hour Society. Anyone walking around with even half an eye open will realize that there is a social change going on bigger than simply electronic shopping. High street shops are open later, people are eating out at tables on the pavement, working hours are more flexible and there is life on the street after dark. The UK is beginning to develop a café society similar to that in mainland Europe but new to the strait-laced streets of British cities. This change includes a new way of looking at the time constraints and the divides in our lives. There are new relationships between the time spent at home, at work and at leisure. The 24 Hour Society is one of those all-enveloping changes that profoundly influence so many aspects of the way we live.

The old time-markers – night and day, morning, noon and night, weekday and weekend – are losing their relevance. We are having to come to terms with a world that is always open. While a 24 Hour Society may be exaggerating the new developments, it is a useful shorthand for the changes underway. It is unlikely that everything will be open all the time in any reasonably near future and the extended hours society is a better but less evocative phrase. However, 24 Hours serves as a metaphor for a different type of world. It is not just that shops are open later. It is about removing constraints. This book considers why that world is coming about and what it will mean.

The book's genesis was in 1995 when it became obvious to me that the 24 Hour Society was one of those super-tanker trends. It was coming and there was no way it could be stopped. As I wrote in a report,

> as the distinctions between night and day and weekend and weekday are increasingly eroded what does it mean for the way people use their time? Will work patterns, shopping habits, leisure activities and friendship networks alter? Will the time tyranny of institutions that rule our lives such as schools or colleges change as they and doctors, dentists, pharmacists, town halls and other services are made to adapt to the needs of the new, more demanding citizens? As we move from separate day-time and night-time economies to a seamless total hours society how will shops, utilities, service organisations, restaurants, hairdressers and a myriad of other businesses large and small respond to these profound changes?[1]

British Telecom (BT) and First Direct sponsored research into the 24 Hour Society by myself and associates at the Future Foundation to help answer those questions. We ran focus groups and quantitative surveys with the public and businesses. Some of the research is reported here. But the main aim of this book is to place the moves to a 24 Hour Society in the broader context of our search to find a new relationship with time.

The 24 Hour Society is a result of the breakdown of the time structures that constrained our lives. The clock-driven society in which we live imposes stresses and strains that are increasingly destroying the balance between work and home, between rest and play. New patterns of activity have to be found reflecting new economic and workplace trends. We must come to terms with the new mantra of flexibility and the new opportunities for consumption and activity offered by round-the-clock society. In essence, we have to learn to adapt to an inexorable extension of our days and a blurring of the temporal lines.

Chapters 1 and 2 describe the 24 Hour Society and why it is coming about. While most of the examples are from the UK, it is a world-wide phenomenon driven by common pressures on people's time. Many of these time pressures derive from the change in family structures brought about by the increasing involvement of women in the workplace. We are finding it difficult to cope with the consequences for the balance between work and home that arise from the wholly laudable progression towards sex equality at work.

Underlying the change in the nature and composition of the workforce is the shift from male-dominated manufacturing industry to service industries resulting from new technologies. Chapters 3 and 4 consider how this has come about and the way in which 'consumer culture emerged in the often unacknowledged social decision to direct industrial innovation toward producing unlimited quantities of goods rather than leisure.'[2] We now have an insatiable desire to consume which prevents us from down-shifting and accepting more time in return for a less materialist life. Technology also leads to an increasing globalization of the economy, which imposes a different rhythm on the workplace determined by the need to integrate production and delivery of goods and services in time with a global system. This leads to pressures on employees' time as they have to work locally in a global pattern.

To cope with the new social systems in which we live we have to find a new relationship with time. Chapters 5 and 6 explore the differences between the clock time that came in with the Industrial Revolution and the natural time that preceded it. Although we live by clock time we hanker for natural time and the fluid and dynamic nature of the 24 Hour Society is an attempt to synthesize these two views of time. While we can improve our own time management, structural solutions to our time problems have to be sought. Some answers may be found by enabling individuals to construct their own time schedules and edit their own time patterns in a 24 Hour Society but as a quid pro quo, far more flexibility in working hours is required from everyone.

Some of the answers to finding a new relationship with time may come from biology. Chapter 7 questions why we need to sleep and if so how much and when. New work in chronobiology points to the possibility of altering the circadian rhythms that influence our periods of wake and rest and the means by which they may be manipulated to suit our purposes. Chapter 8 considers the current extent and effects of night-working and offers suggestions for coping with changing schedules and shift patterns.

In recent years, round-the-clock delivery companies that promise to deliver your parcel anywhere by 10.30 the next morning have changed the logistical base of many organizations. In effect, these companies provide a flying inventory that enables even small companies to operate globally. The couriers of this world perform a role in space that effectively shrinks transcontinental transactions to local deliveries. Telecoms companies have shrunk distances and opened up new means of round-the-clock working through the use of the telephone, fax, email, ISDN, answerphone and the Internet. Chapter 9 looks at the way companies are beginning to realize that the always-open company offering continuous access performs a role in time that gives it a competitive advantage. Examples include giant companies such as Tesco at one end of the size spectrum and a two-man barber shop at the other.

The 24 hour city is a shorthand for a new way of organizing urban living that is more in keeping with the world of the twenty-first century than the one we are leaving behind. The cities of the future will be hubs in a global network, intimately connecting the solitary individual to the collective billions on the planet. While many cities claim to be 24 hour, none as yet are. Several models are discussed and Chapter 10 ends with the suggestion that the introduction of the 24 hour city and the need to integrate the work of planners, architects, retailers, manufacturers, schools and colleges among others may be a key role for the new mayors.

The last chapter discusses some of the pros and cons of the 24 Hour Society. My own conviction is that provided we move towards it in a way that precludes loading all the work outside conventional hours onto one section of society, and instead introduce flexibility in work hours into all strata of society, then its effect will be beneficial. It will not only help to reduce the crippling time pressures on many people but also reinvigorate urban living.

In his seminal book, *Night as Frontier*, the American sociologist Murray Melbin compared the night to the frontier in the Old West.[3] He saw an analogy between a shortage of land then and the shortage of time now. 'A frontier', according to Melbin, 'is a new source of supply for resources that people want for subsistence or profit. It is a safety valve for people who feel confined.' In that sense, a frontier divides a society with a scarce supply of a certain resource from a territory that can provide that resource. In the case of the Old West it was land: opening the frontier provided millions of acres for farms and homesteads and led to the great western migration in the USA.

When time is the scarce resource, as it is at the end of the twentieth century for many groups in society, then the night is a source of supply. It seems to be a human characteristic that whenever we come up against scarcity in our environment we expand the frontiers. By colonizing the night through the 24 Hour Society we cannot create time but we can provide the means to use the available time more effectively so that we can free ourselves from the coiled grip of the time squeeze.

1 The future is in Bolton?

It is a sin to go to bed the same day you get up

1920s New York mayor Jimmy Walker[1]

A 200 acre, windy site in the middle of nowhere is not the most obvious source of the beginnings of a social revolution. Yet 5 miles outside Bolton, off Junction 6 of the M61, is the future – Middlebrook. At first sight this retail and leisure park looks much like dozens of others, except for the new hi-tech fantasy of Bolton Wanderers football club dominating the sky-line. Sitting next to the spectacular Reebok stadium, named after one of the club's sponsors, is the most innovative leisure and retail development in Britain. This is where the 24 Hour Society is being born.

In Bolton? Apart from the footballer Nat Lofthouse, England's heroic post-war centre forward, not much has come out of Bolton since the 1940s. It is a nice enough town, with some solid Victorian municipal buildings and streets, but its heyday has long gone from the days of cotton and textiles. Now it is struggling to find a role, dominated by Manchester just a few miles up the road.

Somewhat brazenly (and some would say risibly) the town has declared itself a 24 hour city. It has a specific policy for the evening economy and a clear idea of how attitudes to time are changing. Even young Italians fly over to rave the night away at the town's largest club. Attempts are being made to nurture some kind of evening economy in the town centre and its shopping parade, but it is at Middlebrook where the main action is taking place.

The site was dormant for years, part owned by Bolton Wanderers and the town council as well as other smaller interests. It was marketed as an indus-trial site but the one thing the north-west was not short of was industrial sites. What it lacked was manufacturing industry. There simply was not enough of it about. After a fairly fruitless few years, a local property developer was brought in to try and get something off the ground. Enter visionary number one, Stan Annison, managing director of the commercial division of a local property company, the Emerson Group.

Annison has been in the property game since 1962, when he left school at 16. He has the smooth patina of the businessman who has made it big, but there is little he has not seen or done in property development and the street-wise 16 year old is still there under the gold watch. He is convinced that the future in Bolton is going to be different.

Doodling on a pad, Annison sketched out the way town planners used to think and to a large extent still do. In any town, the shops and municipal offices would be in the centre, surrounded by a sector for factories, another for offices, with some sports and leisure over here and residential areas over there. In this way, the planners, councillors, architects and government zoned the cake and decided how people would live their lives. It was a particular picture of the world, which translated the moral view of the powers-that-be as to how people should live into a physical reality. Not only was there a place for everything and everything kept its place, but also there was a time for everything and everything had its time.

As car ownership grew and people became more mobile, however, they began refusing to live their lives in the planners' neatly separate packages. The old demarcations were broken down. When today's customers want something they want it now. If now happens to be 9 p.m or 11 p.m., then so be it. If people want to see a film they want to see it at a time that suits them rather than the cinema. If they are shopping in the afternoon and want a meal at 3 p.m. or 5 p.m., they want somewhere to be open nearby.

People live joined-up lives where the distinctions between morning, afternoon, evening and night are starting to go as surely as the distinctive butchers, fishmongers, delicatessen and greengrocers' shops have merged into the supermarket. Work is now flexible, which means the old-style 9 to 5 job with weekends off is becoming a thing of the past, almost a minority pursuit. When a bookshop offers supermarket-style baskets to its customers and is open 8 a.m. until 11 p.m. six days a week, when a supermarket is also a bank and is open round the clock, and when the home can double up as a workplace, in 24 hour contact on-line with anywhere in the world, then as Dorothy said in the *Wizard of Oz*, we are not in Kansas anymore.

Stan Annison recognized that people wanted something different. His plan was to build a retail and leisure park that complemented rather than determined the way people lived. But it was going to cost around £100 million to develop both the Reebok stadium and the Middlebrook site. Some of the money would come from his company Emerson, so he had to be right. And the park would be built just at the time when the government was clamping down on out-of-town sites.

Until 1996, the two conventional anchor tenants of a large out-of-town park were a department store and a supermarket. With these on board a developer had the confidence to push the construction buttons. But with the change in government thinking and the restrictions on out-of-town development it became far harder to find these tenants. Planning permission for out-of-town department stores dried up as the local authorities tried to protect and conserve town centres. New supermarkets tended to be relocations. Annison had to find another anchor and from that need, a social revolution was born.

Enter visionary number two. Millard Ochs is the boss of the massive Warner cinema chain. Annison persuaded Ochs that a leisure-based site could work and that a cinema could be a perfect anchor tenant. Ochs agreed and allowed the new Warner Village multiplex to be built set back from the overall frontage, at the end of a restaurant 'mini-mall'. This is not the Storming of the Bastille but it was a UK first for Warner and its significance is far deeper than it seems. Ochs realized that the future lay in integrating activities. In the entertainment world it is called 'eatertainment'. People do not just want to go and see a film. They want to see a film, then maybe have a drink or a meal, or even do some shopping. They want to join up their lives. And they want to do it at times that suit them. Bolton Council chipped in with the new thinking, giving the cinema Britain's only 24 hour licence.

What Annison was doing, although he did not fully appreciate it at the time, was building a new small town. Only he was doing it back to front to suit consumer demand. The first priorities were the leisure and shopping facilities, the new heart of modern existence. Then industrial capacity was added when Hitachi built a 120 employee hi-tech factory on the site. The Royal Bank of Scotland established a call centre in another corner to handle inquiries about financial products. A hotel was built and some adjacent land used for housing. In less than a year a site employing 3,000 people was built; when the housing and the latest development, a tennis complex, is complete around 5,000 people will live and work at Middlebrook. All it needs is a church and there have been enquiries about that.

Annison's plan of having a football stadium next to a retail park recognized the role of leisure, including shopping, in modern life. Football is not the new rock 'n' roll but it has become a family entertainment and a major part of the leisure industry. The social revolution will be fully under way when the ritual of the 3 p.m. Saturday kick-off and its connotations of cloth-capped working men thronging the terraces is finally substituted by a Saturday evening kick-off. Then we will know Britain has fully switched from a manufacturing to a service economy. Before that happens, kick-off times may be dictated by global media companies that might own not only the TV stations but also the clubs themselves.

The twelve-screen Warner cinema at Middlebrook opens until late and has experimented with all-night opening, the vast Co-op travel shop shuts at 8 p.m. and the bowling alley closes around midnight. Middlebrook is not yet a 24 hour site, more like a 15–16 hour one. Whether literally or metaphorically a round-the-clock site, it is the pointer of things to come.

When he needs cheering up, Annison counts the people coming to Middlebrook. It attracts 140,000 visitors a week and is geared towards what used to be called blue-collar families. In that sense it is democratic. It won't please the architectural purists but it makes a real and beneficial difference to people's time-pressured lives. The restaurants may be the themed offers from the big breweries and the shops are not mould-breaking, but the late opening and the overall mix make it easier for people to organize their time and their lives. And the formula is being copied around Britain. Annison is handling the commercial development of the Lowry gallery in Manchester's Salford Quays and has made sure that a cinema will anchor the development.

The change is not just taking place in the North of England, it is easy to see the 24 Hour Society happening all around the UK. Shops open longer, service stations operate round the clock, radio and TV broadcast through the night, libraries open on Sundays, and most pubs might be open to midnight soon. There is talk of London's Soho becoming a 24 hour zone with pubs open round the clock.

Official evidence backs the claim that the UK is moving into a 24 hour world. The National Grid has recorded an increase in electricity usage between 6 p.m. and 10 p.m. since the late 1980s and attributes this to shops staying open later and staying lit.[2] BT has noted an increase in telephone traffic at night. While total residential calls have increased by two-thirds since 1989, call volumes at midnight are up 150 per cent, rising to 250 per cent just after 2 a.m. and to 400 per cent around 4.30 a.m.[3] These night-time call increases are from a low base but are indicative of the change. Other evidence from the National Travel Survey shows that there has been a small but important increase in the percentage of 'shopping trips' moving to later in the day and the weekend.[4] For the supermarkets and do-it-yourself (DIY) retailers Sunday can be the busiest day on an hour-by-hour basis.

The huge fifty check-out ASDA store that relocated to the Middlebrook site closes at 11 p.m six days a week. It is open for the maximum six hours on Sunday. Late night supermarkets are now common in Britain and *de rigueur* in most towns. Many are open till 10 p.m. most nights and through the night on Friday. Tesco has sixty-three stores open 24 hours five days a week. Late night supermarket shoppers predictably include doctors, nurses, manual workers, croupiers, foreign exchange traders and all manner of shift workers.

There are also many surprises. People in wheelchairs shop late because they have more room to manoeuvre along the aisles. Parents with young babies find that when the child wakes in the night, one remedy is to put the infant in a car where the motion soon sends it back to sleep. Rather than pace anxiously around the bedroom, one or both parents can go to the super-market with the child, who sleeps through the shopping experience. The late night stores are also popular with young people and ASDA has gone as far as promoting singles nights. Tesco found that 6 a.m. on a Saturday morning, when the children are still asleep, was a favourite time for younger working mothers. Instead of opening for what Tesco thought would be the odd top-up shopper, scores of younger women have chosen to buy the full family shop in the early morning.

Although it seems shopping has always been like this, in the UK shopping hours were deregulated only in 1994. The Shops Act 1994 changed the retail picture and it is not only the large supermarkets who are looking at ways of further extending their evening and night-time activity.

For many years the industry wisdom was that food and petrol did not mix. Petrol stations sold a few confectionery items but since the 1980s, under competitive pressure from the supermarkets, who now sell more than half of the UK's petrol, all the main petrol companies are developing a shopping format. Shell has been the pioneer, building Shell Select shops in 850 service stations in the UK. The shops sell up to 3,000 product lines in food and drink, newspapers and magazines, treats, gifts and flowers and 'top-up' shopping. Over 80 per cent of the shops are open round the clock. Most of the customers are convenience or distress purchasers and are relatively insensitive to price as the items are simply added on to the petrol bill.

Shell's research found that 17 million people now shop at night; 1 million say that they can shop only after 10 p.m. Another survey found that nearly a quarter of shoppers do their main grocery shop after 6 p.m. Perhaps more significantly, 30 per cent of those aged between 18 and 24 who buy a main grocery shop go in the evening. If any substantiation were needed that this is a developing trend among the young, market researchers Nielsen Homescan found that 58 per cent of young people without children say that they would go shopping at night.

It is not just the retail and leisure industries that are reinventing themselves. Education is also adapting to the changes in society. In Gateshead, a new concept in bringing education to people was set up in 1996. Learning World is a joint venture between Gateshead College and the University of Sunderland. It is one of the most interesting new developments in the breakdown of the temporal distinctions in people's lives.

The site has been built next to the huge retail complex, the Metro Centre. The Centre, which is open from 9 a.m. until 9 p.m. employs around 6,500 people and is visited by about 600,000 customers a week. The 6,500 employees provide a potential pool of students for Learning World. Visitors to the Centre can shop, eat, go to the cinema and possibly do a bit of learning, all at the same time. Learning World is open from 9 a.m. until 9 p.m. six days a week – the same hours as the retail centre – and it also opens on Sundays. It even looks more like a retailer than a college, both inside and out. To meet the demands of its students, who often work complex shift patterns, multiple sessions of courses are on offer so that someone who would miss three weeks because of a shift change will not miss out. The pool of part-time lecturers often prefer working at 'off-peak' times and at weekends, enabling the timetable to have a much-needed flexibility. Learning World is busy in the mornings, quiet in the afternoons and busy again in the evenings – just like the retail centre.

It would be stretching the point to suggest that Learning World has cracked the problems of turning Britain into a Learning Society, but the idea is catching on. The new Bluewater retail park near Dartford in Kent will have a Learning Shop run in conjunction with North West Kent College. Other retail and leisure parks are likely to introduce their own versions in this attempt to tailor learning to people's flexible lifestyles.

Flexibility has also begun to invade the university world, notoriously resistant to radical change. Students at Bath University can use the UK's only 24-hour main university library any time except Saturday nights. The library used to shut at midnight each night (and still does in July and August), but library managers found during term time they were turning out forty or more students at the witching hour. By the 9 a.m opening the following day there would be queues at the entrance.

The 24 hour opening of the library was intended to reassert the library's key role as the centre of the university. As the Vice-Chancellor explained,

> Fifty years ago the Library was the place where students spent a lot of time poring over books. Now it is a place where they not only do their homework and write their papers on computer but can also have group discussions and meet socially. A lot of the time the centre will be lightly used, but if we can do it at reasonable cost, we can let students and academics be driven by their schedule, not an artificial schedule driven by the University.

Typically, about 120–160 students use the library between midnight and 6 a.m. but before exams around 500 crowd in to do their last-minute swotting.

Compared to what is happening in the further education area, most schools are still tied to the time disciplines of the past. Legh Vale Primary School in Cheshire is an exception. It provides a breakfast club before school and an after-school club at 3.30 p.m. The school is open until 9 p.m. four nights a week. But the later times are not for the children. While some stay on after school until 5.30 p.m., the evening classes that are run in conjunction with nearby St Helen's College are for adults. One-third of parents with primary age children would like schools to be open outside the conventional hours of 9 a.m. to 3.30 p.m., but most primary school classrooms are open for only 15 per cent of the 168 hours available. Secondary schools are only slightly better, managing 17 per cent.

There have been several attempts at creating 24 hour schools to provide an integrated service for children and parents and an open-all-hours learning resource for the local community. In the late 1970s, the then Inner London Education Authority rejected one such imaginative scheme in the London Borough of Lambeth and while some other local authorities have tinkered with the issue, few have gone beyond the laudable but grossly inadequate efforts of schools such as Legh Vale.

Murfreesboro town council in Tennessee has shown how it could be done. The Murfreesboro schools have one of the most comprehensive extended-opening programmes in the USA. In 1986, Murfreesboro announced that one primary school would be open from 6 a.m. to 6 p.m. and parents would pay for the extended-day services. Four students showed up. Within two years, public demand forced the concept to be adopted by every primary school in the city. In 1996, 50 per cent of the city's 5,000 primary school students made use of the programme on any given day, all on a voluntary basis on the parents' part.

The secondary schools in Murfreesboro offer educational services from 8 a.m. till 5.30 p.m., extended services before school from 6 a.m. and after school until 7 p.m. Extended services are available five days a week, fifty-two weeks a year. In principle it is possible to have a two-shift school. The first shift would run from 8 a.m. to 2 p.m. with an optional breakfast at 7.30 a.m. and lunch at 1 p.m. The afternoon shift would be from 1.30 p.m until 6.30 p.m with a break for tea and an optional supper. This scheme allows for more intensive use of the buildings, providing parents with much needed flexibility in choosing school hours that complement their work times.

As the Murfreesboro example shows, while Britain is just getting used to a 24 hour world, the USA is 'further down the road' and is 'a work-all-the-time society driven by consumer and commercial pressure'.[5] New York is held up as the archetypal 24 hour city. Manhattan most definitely is. In

Manhattan different groups live at different times. From 6 a.m. to 7 p.m. the city serves the commuters, who double the size of the resident population. From 6 p.m. to midnight the local residents knock off from work, and support the restaurants, cafés and bars. At 1 a.m., the younger club crowd, especially gay men, emerge and populate the late-night clubs and 24 hour restaurants. Then the chefs finish work and go to their favourite restaurants.

Unlike most American cities such as Atlanta or St Louis, which empty out by 11 p.m., there is pedestrian traffic at all hours in New York. And, of course, the subways never stop running. However, they are a bit creepy after 2 a.m. For passengers travelling late at night, most stations have a central gathering spot bordered in yellow, which encourages people to wait in a group and then use the central cars of the train near the conductor.

In *A Geography of Time*, Robert Levine used the time it took to buy a stamp at a post office as one of the comparative indicators of the pace of life in different countries. He also used the average speed of pedestrians in downtown city areas and the accuracy of public clocks as a measure of the concern with the pace of life. Surprisingly, Switzerland turned out to have the fastest pace of life; Britain came in sixth place and the USA ranked sixteenth. In a separate survey of US cities, using walking speed, bank transactions, the percentage of people wearing watches and the talking speed of counter clerks in post offices, Levine rated Boston top, followed by Buffalo and New York.[6] Chicago came sixteenth.

Post offices around the world are notorious for their bureaucratic approach, which is why Levine chose them. As if to buck the trend, Chicago's post offices are extending their opening hours. Since June 1998, Chicago's main post office at 433 W. Harrison is open 24 hours a day, seven days a week. Three other post offices open on Sundays for five hours. The extended hours were the result of a customer survey that found in many instances opening times were a primary concern for the customer.

Some UK local authorities are running extended-hours pilot projects, but generally Britain is behind other western countries despite the fact that restrictive opening times are one of the public's primary concerns. A glimpse of what might be in the world of local and national government can be seen in the Australian state of Victoria. By the year 2000, Victoria citizens will be able to register their car on-line, pay state and local bills and deal with

government 24 hours a day at home or in the workplace. The idea is to provide services based around people's life events. Victoria has a Land Channel,
Business Channel and Citizen's Channel among others that enable people to
deal easily with the authorities without having to deal with different depart-
ments. The key point of the system is to enable citizens to easily access government services without the need to understand the underlying structure of
government and how it works.

While the Victoria system is a state of the art world leader, Temple in
Texas operates a more modest 24 hour town hall information system that
enables citizens with touch-tone telephones to dial in any time and access
286 topics, ranging from the agenda for the next city council meeting to
smoking regulations in public buildings. The topics are accessed using a
three digit code chosen from the directory mailed out with the water bills.
Up to a thousand topics can be put on the system. A fax-back system allows
callers to get applications and permits that can then be faxed back to the
town hall.

The private sector has been paying more attention to the public's needs.
In the UK, personal banking was revolutionized in the mid-1970s, when the
first Automated Telling Machines (ATMs) were installed. Telephone banking started in Britain in 1989, initially with First Direct. Now, all the main
banks and building societies offer variants of a 24 hour service. Hardly
anyone phones First Direct in the middle of the night. But only half the
weekday calls are made between 9 a.m and 5 p.m. Customers tend to start
using the service at 6 a.m and 20 per cent of calls are made in the evening
between 6 p.m. and 11 p.m.[7]

One welcome American import to Britain is the ultra-late opening book-
store. The Borders shop on London's Oxford Street is open from 8 a.m.
(breakfast is available in the in-store café) to 11 p.m. six days a week and
from 11 a.m. to 6 p.m. on Sundays. Borders is following the UK path pio-
neered by Waterstone's, which is still likely to be the last shop to close on the
traditional British high street.

An American phenomenon which has not yet crossed the Atlantic is the
all-night chemist. Some independent chemists are open until midnight and
there are twenty or so Boots stores open in out-of-town retail sites until
9 p.m. A trial 24 hour opening of a Boots store in Leeds railway station,

initiated by the local health authority, may lead to similar developments at other mainline stations. But nobody is so far thinking of introducing the drive-through pharmacy or all-night dentists. A private drop-in general practitioner (GP) service does exist at nine MediCentres. Four of them are in London mainline rail stations, another is on Oxford Street (London) and four are based in Sainsbury stores in the Midlands and North of England. The rail station MediCentres are open from 7 a.m to 9 p.m. during the week and 9 a.m. to 9 p.m. at the weekend. The store-based centres are open during the shop hours of 8 a.m. to 10 p.m. in the week and 10 a.m. to 4 p.m. on Sundays.

The National Health Service (NHS) plans to supply a 24 hour medical helpline service to all parts of Britain by the year 2000. NHS Direct provides instant telephone access to expert advice from nurses 24 hours a day 365 days a year. In just one month between May and June 1998 the three pilot areas took over 4,000 calls from members of the public seeking urgent help. The second wave of pilots includes GP practices among the service providers and it is not too difficult to envisage a properly integrated service that allows primary care to be delivered day and night more effectively than the current GP call-out service. If limited prescribing rights are allowed to NHS Direct staff and participating pharmacists, then a new pattern of night-time primary healthcare could develop.

Where might it stop? It is easy to see the demand for late night and early morning shops, petrol stations, restaurants, pubs, supermarkets, car dealerships, overnight car servicing, television and cinema. Next in line will be personal service activities such as hairdressers, dry cleaners, doctors, chiropodists, dentists and accountants. The Japanese have discovered a demand for late-night massages. In Tokyo, some shops offer relaxation – particularly through massage – to both men and women around the clock. The charge for a fifteen-minute rub-down is 1,500 yen (about £7) and many working women call in on their way home after putting in overtime. In the early morning, the main customers are men on their way to work.

The move to a 24 Hour Society will gradually encompass public transport, town halls and central governments as the latter build interactive systems into their telephones and web-sites. Eventually the whole of Britain might beat to a 24 hour clock.

2 The demand for more time

Let me talk to you about my generation... We built a new popular culture, transformed by colour TV, Coronation Street and the Beatles. We enjoy a thousand material advantages over any previous generation, and yet we suffer a depth of insecurity and spiritual doubt they never knew.

Tony Blair, Labour Party Conference 1995

It is clear that some kind of 24 Hour Society is evolving, but who and what are driving it along? Who needs the flexibility offered by a round-the-clock world where everything is open all the time? Whose time demands are being met? And what are the factors behind the consumer demand?

One group clearly articulating their demand for a 24 hour world are the young. Surveys show that three-quarters of British 18–24 year olds feel that their lives would be a lot easier if everything was open all the time, something that would probably be echoed by young people everywhere. Young people have always had the energy to burn the candle at both ends. Although some teenagers still complain they have nothing to do, a combination of liberalized drinking laws and new-style bars, clubs, restaurants and coffee houses have created an entertainment culture that does rock around the clock. *Time Out*, the London listings magazine, regularly publishes articles showing how to party continuously for 24 hours by going from club to club in the capital.

Groups of somewhat bedraggled young Parisians are a frequent early Saturday morning feature at London's Waterloo Station as they wait for a Eurostar train to take them home. Some will go straight to work. They come to London on Friday evenings and spend the night at a nearby club. It happens every weekend throughout the UK. Young people come by train and plane from all over Europe for a flavour of the British club scene.

In cities around the UK, young singles are creating their own version of a 24 Hour Society. On a warm evening the bustling, heaving mass of bodies on

Islington's Upper Street makes it impossible to see where the cafés, bars and restaurants end and the pavement begins. It is a scene emulated in Leeds' Calls area, Manchester's Castlefield, Cardiff's Mill Lane, Brighton's Arches and the Strip along Whiteladies Road in Bristol.

New female-friendly bars, such as All Bar One from the Bass chain, are being developed, to appeal particularly to younger working women. The burgeoning coffee houses such as Seattle Coffee Company and Coffee Republic with their younger clientele have become ubiquitous since the mid-1990s. The availability of croissants and café latte at 7 a.m. in a City of London coffee shop is a sign that something really has changed.

However, working women in the 25–45 bracket, especially those with children, have little time to spend in bars or coffee shops. They are the main victims of the time squeeze. The working mother is one of the busiest people on earth, whether she has a partner or not. This group of women works a first shift at the office, factory, shop or hospital and then faces a second shift at home. Since the late 1980s there has been a huge rise in the numbers of women with small children who work. In 1997 55 per cent of women whose youngest dependent child was under 5 worked. In 1987 the figure was 42 per cent. These are the people who are at the forefront in demanding a new way to edit the time in their lives.[1] They are the ones who can most benefit from a 24 Hour Society.

There has been a long-standing and steady increase in the numbers of working women. As recently as 1971, just over 45 per cent of women in the 25–34 age group, the key child-rearing years, were at work. In 1998 it was a little over 71 per cent and likely to rise. After Denmark, the UK has the highest female participation rate in employment in the EU, mainly due to the large numbers of women in Britain in part-time jobs. Women form more than half the workforce in Liverpool, Glasgow, Bristol, Manchester and Sheffield.

These women are not all employed in part-time, low-paid jobs. There are now more female solicitors and female pharmacists under 30 than male ones. One-third of managers and administrators are women, as are one-third of health professionals and just over a quarter of buyers, brokers and sales representatives. These are the groups that articulate the time demands on women – 86 per cent say they never have enough time to get things done. Women who work full-time report that they have 10 per cent less time in the late 1990s than they did in the 1980s while men say they have 4 per cent less time.[2] Nine out of ten full-time women workers say that they do not have enough time to do everything they need to do, while seven out of ten workers, particularly young people and women, want more flexible hours.

The stereotypical family with a male breadwinner, full-time housewife and 2.4 children disappeared long ago. But the balance of responsibilities between the sexes has yet to reflect the new social order. The family structure, even though it has changed, is still problematic for employed family members. Part of the difficulty is that many well-paid jobs have implicitly assumed the existence of a stay-at-home spouse who is always available for child-care or caring for elderly relatives and can free the employee of domestic duties such as cooking, cleaning, shopping or doing laundry. These positions are called *jobs with wives*.

This has been seen in stark relief in Japan. In 1997, a Japanese woman took her husband to court, having left him on the grounds that she was tired of not only doing her own job but also acting as an unpaid servant in the home. The 31-year-old woman had a full-time job and had made it clear to her husband that in order for her to fulfil her work and domestic chores they would have to move closer to her job. She was not even asking for him to do more in the home, just to help her out by cutting down her journey time. The couple saw nine homes and the husband rejected them all. The court ruled in her favour, something of a revolution in a fiercely patriarchal society.

Japanese men do very little when it comes to sharing housework. If the husband is the sole income earner of a married couple, on average he will do about four minutes of housework a day. Should his wife also work he increases his contribution to five minutes a day.

Before we in the west get too complacent, domestic and work-sharing arrangements in Britain are none too enlightened. If a husband and wife are both working the same hours, on average the woman does at least an extra nine hours a week of housework.[3] This is broadly true throughout Europe and North America. For full-time employed women, the second shift can involve up to eight different tasks a day: cooking, cleaning, washing, ironing and so on. Men who do housework usually manage two tasks at most. A US study found that in a family with three children, working mothers typically spent ninety hours on paid and unpaid work, while men spent sixty hours.

While men may protest that they do their share, another survey found that though 63 per cent of fathers felt that they did as much housework as their partners and 54 per cent said they did as much parenting, only 43 per cent of the women agreed that their male partners shared the housework equally. Less than one-third said the men shared parenting responsibilities.

Women work the second shift

Working the second shift, not only do women work longer, but also they have a harder time adjusting between home and work. When men get home, they can relax, watch TV, even play with the children and get them wound up just before bedtime. When women arrive home from work, they face a whole new set of responsibilities, from making doctor's appointments to supervising homework, finding dinner money and doing the laundry.[4] So it is hardly surprising that working mothers are keenest on doctors and pharmacies opening early and closing late. They would also like to see flexibility in the timing of the school day to meet their needs.

The demand from working women for more flexible opening times for services has resulted in 125 Italian cities adopting what they call 'city time'.[5] Law 142 on local autonomy, enacted in 1990, gives city mayors the ability 'to co-ordinate opening hours in a way that reflects the needs of users'. The female mayor of Modena led the way in providing one-stop centres for a range of council services so that citizens did not waste time having to deal with different offices. Her time-saving measures were deliberately targeted at women.

THE TEACHER

A 24 hour post office and late-opening dry cleaners might not make her life complete but both would go some way to solving Meryl Davies' time problems.

Meryl is deputy head of a large (1,500 pupil) comprehensive school in south London. She also has three children under 7, a husband who is a TV producer and a house still needing building work. She is a classic example of a busy working mother.

Her working day starts at around 7.15 a.m. when she leaves for school. She is back home twelve hours later. 'Sometimes, it is basic survival. I just have to keep going all the time.' It is quite an admission from a high-energy woman who has never minded being busy and working long hours.

'Fortunately I have a live-in nanny who looks after the kids. There is no way I could do it otherwise.' But it is still not easy. Teachers tend to be chained to the school. Once there in the morning they seldom go outside until they leave for home. So there is no time in the day to do any shopping or get small things done, like shoe repairs, or having her hair cut.

> I used to enjoy going to the hairdresser and spending a couple of hours there but I can't do that now. And I don't want to do it at the weekend as I prefer being with the children. A woman comes to my home and does it. Andy, my husband, does the grocery shopping on a Saturday evening at about 8 p.m. The late night opening really makes a difference to us as we get the Saturday and Sunday to do things as a family. The kids don't want to be hauled round a supermarket.

When Meryl Davies gets time off, when her mother comes to stay for example, her idea of luxury is being able to potter around the shops. In reality, she ends up doing the domestic jobs that usually she has no time for. Heaven for her would be sitting on a beach in Greece.

And the post office? After visiting her mother in Oswestry, the family went on holiday to France, stopping off in London to pick up a few things including an E111 form.

> We had to get the E111 healthcare form stamped. It was in the afternoon and I could not be sure that I would find a post office that was open. I was starting to panic. Luckily we got to London just in time to find one. But it was close. You don't need late-opening post offices all the time, but when you need one you really do need it. That and dry cleaners would be a help. And a dentist who was open late. And a doctor.

While 80 per cent of British working couples with children feel that they are often under time pressure in everyday life, men recognize the imbalance in time use when questioned at length. It is clear that equity in the distribution of work and domestic time between men and women would be one way of alleviating women's current time sickness. Although a quarter of men claimed that they would rather look after the home than go to work, evidence of the domestic New Man of the 1990s is hard to come by. Occasionally, this much-vaunted New Man was sighted. He first appeared in the early 1990s in advertisements for everything from cars to yoghurts. Sensitive and caring, he was supposed to break with the past. He was able and even eager to help with raising the children, cooking, doing the shopping as well as the DIY. New Man was supposedly the answer to every woman's dream.

But before the magazine covers were printed, New Man metamorphosed into New Lad. New Man may well have possessed all the right intentions and skills, but faced with the reality of child-rearing he soon retreated into the learned helplessness that generations of men have discovered is the tactic to use when threatened with the deprivation of their own free time. Ask a man to iron and he will try. But in many cases it is not long before the woman says, 'You are taking so long it will be quicker to do it myself.' And she does.

Doing better and feeling worse

While working mothers bear the brunt of the time pressure, 25–54-year-old full-time working parents, both male and female, are caught in a time trap. Most of them have never had it so good, yet they feel lousy, as Tony Blair suggested in his 1995 speech. A 1996 Gallup poll found that more than three-quarters of the sample interviewed believed that people enjoyed less peace of mind than they used to, with only 3 per cent saying the opposite.[6] The condition has been called Doing Better and Feeling Worse.

The British are certainly doing better. The UK economy grows in real terms at about 2 per cent a year and doubles roughly every thirty-five years. While the inequalities of income distribution mean that the wealthier groups have received proportionally more of the increase, overall the UK has never been so wealthy. Nine in ten homes in 1998 had at least one colour TV, telephone, washing machine and refrigerator. Two-thirds also had a microwave and video recorder, while one in six had all these plus a dishwasher. British wardrobes and drawers had over three times as many clothes of far better quality than in the 1950s.

Life expectancy at birth is a good indicator of the overall state of health. In the UK it is nudging 75 years for men and 80 for women,[7] an increase of more than 30 years over the century. Compared to 1899 we are almost a different species. On average we may be working an hour or so longer per week than in the late 1980s, but compared to our parents and grandparents we work less and holiday more.

It is salutary to record how US President Lyndon Johnson's mother recalled her youth on a dirt farm in Texas in the early part of the century. She described a woman's burden that had changed little for centuries:

> On washdays, clothes had to be lifted out of the big soaking vats of boiling water on the ends of long poles, the clothes dripping and heavy; the farm filth had to be scrubbed out in hours of kneeling over rough rubboards, hours in which the lye in the home-made soap burned the skin of women's hands; the heavy flatirons had to be continually carried back and forth to the stove for re-heating and the stove had to be continually fed with new supplies of wood – decades later even strong, sturdy farm wives would remember how their backs had ached on washday. [8]

And while William Wordsworth was dreaming of daffodils and taking a somewhat superior view of the rest of humankind's vulgar 'getting and spending', his sister Dorothy did the housework. 'I ironed till dinner-time, sewed till near dark, then pulled a basket of peas and afterwards picked gooseberries,' she wrote. In Dorothy Wordsworth's Victorian times, the work involved in a typical washday was equivalent to swimming five miles of energetic breaststroke.[9]

Electricity liberated women from the sheer physical effort of domestic tasks. In 1881 the Glasgow house of the eminent scientist Lord Kelvin was the world's first to be lit by electricity. During the first half of the twentieth century a huge range of electric household appliances became increasingly common, including washing machines, vacuum cleaners, irons, sewing machines and refrigerators.

In Europe and North America 85 per cent of women polled said that household appliances had contributed a great deal to their quality of life.[10] It is a moot point as to how much time they actually save; there is no satisfactory time-use survey. Some of the time gained has been subverted by higher standards of cleanliness. People wash clothes daily instead of weekly. Children no longer help with the chores but instead are deemed to require unceasing attention from parents, which usually means the mother. Germs have become mortal enemies, to be fought in an unrelenting battle of attrition.

Full-time housewives spend as long on the household chores as full-time housewives always did. As Betty Friedan once said, 'Housewifery expands to fill the time available'.[11] And today there are far fewer full-time housewives: divorce and employment have seen to that. The UK has the highest divorce rate in Europe: nearly half of British marriages end in divorce. Though many women remarry, very few women spend much of their lives as traditional housewives. At the beginning of the twentieth century only half of all 30-year-old women, and less than one-third of 30-year-old women with children, were in work. In 1999, more than two-thirds are working. But few would want to swap places with Mrs Johnson.

In many ways, our lives are far easier. Time-saving technologies have vastly improved the quality and scope of our lives. Distance has been collapsed by the telephone, car, fax machine, courier companies and the Boeing 747. The introduction of vacuum packaging has turned sandwiches from a culinary joke into the UK's favourite fast-food and an instant meal that can be bought almost everywhere. The fridge/freezer and the microwave have made food preparation and cooking a thing of the past. Gourmet meals are now ready in minutes, courtesy of the supermarkets. Finished clothing has put a stop to endless sewing.

Video recorders and digital television effectively shift time and enable us to arrange our viewing to times that suit us. There is a fine line, however, between shifting time and destroying time, the charge usually levelled at the television. Some argue that instead of allowing people to view programmes selectively, video recorders and digital television mean that even more rubbish is watched. Few people with teenage children would challenge that.

Despite these technological miracles and the vastly improved material quality of our lives, survey after survey suggest how bad we feel. Psychologist Oliver James, in his book, *Britain on the Couch*, reports that a variety of studies in the developed world all conclude that psychiatric morbidity, measured by the incidence of depression, the rate of suicide, phobias and panic attacks, was increasing.[12]

So why are we feeling worse? We are finding it very difficult to handle the combination of new family structures, lengthening working hours and the pressures of consumerism. The gap between our aspirations and reality is hard to handle in a society that judges people by what they own as well as what they are. As a society we are anxious, insecure, socially divided and stressed out. A large proportion of the British population believe they are overworked and that life is out of control. Over half the adult population agrees with the statement 'I am often under time pressure in my everyday life', [13] a proportion that rises to 75 per cent among those who are working and looking after a family. Only 17 per cent of adults between 18 and 45 feel free of time pressure in their everyday lives. It is probably no coincidence that the British swallowed £260 million worth of anti-depressant tablets in the twelve months to the end of January 1998, an increase of 23 per cent from the previous year.[14] A Channel 4 survey found that one-third of all women agreed that they never had time for themselves and this rose to 51 per cent of those who worked at least part-time.[15] Time sickness, the feeling of being harried and hurried continually, is the disease of the age. Lack of time has become a common complaint and there is a feeling that it is never possible to relax properly. There is always something else to be done. This is partly because there is so much else that can now be done, but it is also a consequence of the breaking down of barriers between home and work and play.

How did it come to such a pass? After all, if we own twice as much as we did a generation ago but feel that we are working far too hard and need more time, why not simply work fewer hours and consume less? If we worked half the hours, the argument goes, we would still have roughly as much as our parents had. This, in outline, is the nub of the idea put forward by Juliet Schor in her influential book, *The Overworked American*,[16] and it is often heard from advocates of a more sustainable society. It has become known as down-shifting or the idea of living a simpler life that requires less paid work and focuses more attention on the inner self. Attractive as the idea is, it is not going to happen, for reasons that are explained in the following chapters.

In Britain people long ago gave up the drive for shorter hours and opted for money rather than time.

Longer hours

Once the City of London was renowned for its long lunches and leisurely working hours. Now traders, executives, and what are known as client-facing staff in the City of London work upwards of fifty hours a week. These men and women are entrusted with trading millions of pounds of pension funds and other investment money. If they were truck drivers they would be off the road long before the end of their normal working day. It is hardly surprising that very few survive in their jobs past their early thirties. By then they are burnt-out, but their Faustian pact has been made. In return for their enormous pay packets, they give the company body and soul commitment.

Currencies and bonds are now traded globally by telephone and electronic means around the clock. When the New York Stock Exchange closes, the Pacific Exchange in Los Angeles opens. Then the Japanese market opens. Tokyo's closing bell marks the beginning of trading in Johannesburg, followed two hours later by London. Michael Marcus, a famous US trader, described how in the mid-1980s he was trading Deutschmarks: 'I was probably one of the biggest currency traders in the world, including the banks. It was very exhausting because it was already a 24 hour market. When I went to sleep I would have to wake up every two hours to check the market as it opened: Australia, Hong Kong, Zurich and London. It killed my marriage.'[17]

The City of London is an extreme case, but it is part of an overall climate in Britain in which few companies have introduced the means by which the workforce can balance their work and family life.[18] In a survey conducted by the Institute of Management in 1996, only 35 per cent of the managerial respondents felt that they had a good balance between home and work. Working longer hours is cited as one of the prime reasons of time pressure. About 80 per cent suffered some form of stress symptom, mainly caused by unreasonable deadlines.[19] The issue of pressures on family time was highlighted by the high-profile withdrawals of Penny Hughes from the top job in Coca Cola in Europe in 1998 and Linda Kelsey at *She* magazine at the same time, both of them citing the strains of being a working mother. However, this concentration on high-level executives masks the greater time pressures of those who are unable to buy solutions.

THE EXECUTIVE

Antje Schutt flew on a business trip a week before giving birth to her son. Two months later, she, baby Jonas and her husband were in Memphis, USA, at a conference of FedEx top brass. Three months after the birth she was back at work full-time from 7.30 a.m. to 7 p.m.

Her office is close to Frankfurt airport and as managing director of FedEx operations in Germany and Austria she is responsible for a workforce of 850. She is one of the top businesswomen in Europe, and has been voted Female Executive of the Year by *Forbes* magazine. She is a woman with strong views on what is and what is not possible when it comes to time pressures and balancing work and family.

> When you are in a senior executive position it is much easier to balance work and family. There is much more freedom to organize your own activities. It is hourly paid staff who have it much harder, particularly when both parents are working. Their time is very constrained. If you cannot manage to balance your life properly as an executive then you are probably not managing yourself or others very well.

Strong stuff from a woman who admits that she is personally lucky in having a husband who is studying to finish an architecture degree and looks after Jonas in the day. He is some ten years older than her and they decided that he would be the one to give up his career to look after the baby and do something else that he had long wanted to do. As she says, 'If you want a career and family it is important to choose the right partner'. In Germany, unpaid parental breaks can be for up to three years. The idea of the father staying at home while the mother works is becoming less unusual. One male FedEx dispatcher used the three years to gain a PhD.

While no apologist for the 'glass ceiling' in German companies, Schutt acknowledges that men also find it hard to balance their work and family commitments. Some of it is self-imposed as men seem not to raise it as an issue.

> I remember one manager saying once at a meeting that he had to leave as he had a family commitment. I told him fine and that the next day I would tell him what he missed. He was ever so grateful and told me he would not have left early if there had been a male boss. When we discussed it he realized that a male boss may well have been fine about it, it was the manager who was keeping himself within the time-pressure strait-jacket.

Ms Schutt has been balancing her work and home life ever since she joined the company in 1985. She started as a part-time data entry clerk, working an evening shift from 6 p.m. until 10 p.m. This gave her the money to support her daytime studies. 'I had to learn to organize myself but it is easy when you are 24. It helped me later as I learnt how important it is to plan ahead.'

When she knew she was going to have a baby, she gave her boss an action plan showing how she would help out the acting managing director while she was away and how and when she would return to work full-time.

> I suppose I have a CanDo attitude which perhaps comes from working in an American company. European companies still have old-fashioned attitudes about women at work. But if you can show that something is not going to be a problem then it will not become one. I tell my female staff to let me know when they are pregnant as early as possible and not wait for the official dates. That way we can sit and work something out if they want to continue working, such as working from home, job-sharing or whatever is best.

She has already sorted out how to handle things when her husband takes his final examinations. She and Jonas will stay with her parents near Hamburg. Ms Schutt will work in the FedEx Hamburg office, communicating with her Frankfurt office by email and telephone.

Longer hours and its macho overtones are now part of the British business culture. Throughout Britain, men work longer hours than in any other EU country, averaging about forty-three hours a week.

Many EU countries have a different approach to the length of the working week. They still see it as associated with work-sharing as a means of combating high unemployment. An influential West German report suggested that reducing the working week by just one hour and adding a mix of other factors, such as extending schooling by a year, would create an extra 1.3 million jobs.[20] Recently both Italy and France introduced legislation for a maximum thirty-five hour week.

Under the last Conservative government, Britain vigorously resisted any attempts to reduce the working week and famously opted out of the EU working time directive that would limit compulsory work by employees to forty-eight hours a week. The New Labour government, with its penchant for compromise, accepts the directive but does not seem committed to use it as a means of reducing the average working week. While British industrialists rail against the directive, their French counterparts point out that with a population of similar size and far more stringent controls on employment, their economy is some 20 per cent bigger.

For at least the first half of the twentieth century British workers were as keen as their continental counterparts on shortening the working week and increasing leisure time. Professor Gary Cross has explained that there were cultural and economic factors driving this demand in its early stages. The cultural factors lay in different concepts of time. The drive for a shorter working week began in the USA and took its impetus from new immigrants from eastern and southern Europe who were prepared to sacrifice wages for time with their family. To these groups, time for affiliation and association was important. Coincidentally, Taylorism was gaining a grip in the USA, with the introduction of time and motion study to the workplace by Frederick Taylor. The process broke every job into many discrete parts and allocated a time for each part. There was no room in this scheme for social interaction, only a dedication to the clock and an inherent pressure to keep speeding up.[21] The length of the working week was a major industrial battleground.

Cross points out: 'The eight hour day was on the international labour agenda from the spring of 1917; it spread from the US and Russia across

Europe from late 1917 and by mid-1919 had become standard in France and Britain'. It was part of a general approach that time as well as money should reward increases in productivity. In the recession of the 1930s, work-sharing through a reduction in the working week was added to the argument and in 1932, the American Federation of Labour called for a thirty-hour week as an essential work-sharing measure. This idea is still accepted in mainland Europe. The Trades Union Congress (TUC) is still in favour of reducing working hours, but in Britain and in the USA, the demand for a shorter working week effectively dropped off the national agenda in the post-war years.

This happened partly due to an intensifying desire to consume that placed money before time, but also because the call for an ever-shorter week was largely that of male-dominated, blue-collar trade unions. As the composition of the workforce changed and more women became economically active, the focus in Britain has shifted to flexibility of working hours. A TUC document states: 'Flexible working time can give employees greater control over their working lives. An increasing number of agreements show that unions can negotiate more flexibility in working time which helps employees, as well as boosting competitiveness or extending services'.[22] This opens the way for a huge extension in the provision of services outside normal hours.

Some people work long hours because they want to. They may be workaholics or they may find the workplace preferable to being at home. They may be driven individuals. Others do it because of the culture that has developed whereby working longer hours is expected. Job insecurity is a major driver of this longer hours culture. For many people, working longer hours is bound up with the feeling of incessance which is part of modern life. There are no longer the clear boundaries between work and home and leisure. As a result there is the feeling of being 'on call' and never able to fully relax.

Incessant choice

Shirley Conran became famous in 1975, among other things, for saying 'Life is too short to stuff a mushroom'.[23] It was an early commentary on the increasing demands being put on women to become super beings, excelling not only in their jobs, but also in the multiple roles of mother, housewife, lover, shopper and hostess. Now, in the late 1990s, men as well as women have to learn to adapt to the incessant nature of modern living. A similar metaphor could be 'Life is too short to choose a tooth-brush'. A large Boots chemist shop will have over ninety toothbrushes on display; it could take all morning to choose the right one. Choice is overwhelming and it is intensifying. The Gap retail chain revamps its product line every six weeks. Nike introduces a new sports shoe every six weeks.[24]

Incessance is now the way of the world. 'The post-modern era is the period of information, office workers, differentiated structures, globalism and fragmented culture. It is also the era of lost utopias, the end of dominant ideologies. It is the time of incessant choosing.'[25] Being a consumer in an incessant society requires the money and time to participate. It fosters a commercial culture that is dedicated to meeting every consumer want, whether articulated or not. If consumers do not know that they want eight variants of croissants, the marketing people will ensure they will.

Faced with overwhelming choice our instinct is to look for editors. It became fashionable a few years ago to look to clothes shops such as Next to edit our lifestyles. The idea was that rather than spend hours shopping in different stores on a pick 'n' mix basis, we would choose one shop that reflected our tastes and allow that shop to edit the many available choices to suit our style. The idea was seductive and to some extent still works, though it has been overwhelmed by the seemingly irresistible urge to shop as an end in itself.

Individuals edit their own reality. The version and vision that each person has of the world depends on many viewpoints, including the media they consume, the places they go to, the work they do, and the contacts they have. In many ways we are like film editors, putting together in our brains many snippets shot from different cameras at different angles to make a story that we say is reality. We can handle time in this way if we are given the flexibility to do so. This idea of the time editor is fundamental to the 24 hour approach. It requires a change from the 9 to 5 day to a fluid one in which shops, schools, doctors, chemists, workplaces, swimming pools, transport and all the other out-of-home locations in which we live our lives are available from early morning until very late at night. The corollary is that to provide such flexibility, we all have to be prepared to work more flexible hours.

By removing many of the time constraints, we can cope more easily with incessance without having to change our natures and down-shift. Some people are hesitant about what this will mean but as an article in the *Guardian* reassures:

> Just because things are available day and night, doesn't mean you have to do everything all the time. People are afraid of the 24 hour society because they feel they can't do what they've got to do in the time available now. They feel overloaded and see it as having to fit more in, instead of seeing it as doing away with limits and allowing natural time to develop.[26]

We need to edit our time because while we want to have it all and are continually told that 'we deserve it', the desire to have it all runs into the brick wall of lack of time. To solve the problem, some people integrate goals or pursue several simultaneously. For example, the company executive who spends all the time at a son's soccer match conducting business on a mobile phone. Or those who take their children with them on business trips so they can spend time between meetings.[27] Companies respond to these multiple goals on a functional level by providing round-the-clock opening and services to enable customers to schedule their own activities to meet their goals. At a psychic level, they attempt to build into their brands the idea that they satisfy multiple goals. Brands are now offering the idea that they can reduce stress in our lives, as Mars has been doing for decades with its 'Helps you work, rest and play' catch-line.

Editing time to suit our own purposes is the offer made by the 24 Hour Society. It offers the opportunity not of doing it all, but of doing more with less stress.

3 Reshaping our world

We came, we saw, we ran for cover

Fortune magazine, January 1990, on the prospects for the decade

The drive towards a 24 Hour Society is being pushed by technological advance. Technology has not only enabled a new globalization to develop but also changed the nature and culture of work and leisure. It has changed who works, how we work, when and where we work and what work we do.

The key change in western countries resulting from this maelstrom has been the continuing shift from blue-collar manufacturing to service activity. The proportion of the workforce in manufacturing in the UK has shrunk during the twentieth century from around 40 per cent to half that now. Percy Barnevik, the boss of the multinational engineering firm ABB, expects that by 2010 only 10 per cent or so of a modern economy will be in manufacturing as we know it.

The manufacturing world, based on unionized, largely male, family-providing employees working set shift patterns in large workplaces, is very much a thing of the past. But the patterns set by that system still dominate our lives. The changes that have to come from the huge increase in working women, many of them part-time, and the demand by consumers for instant service are battling with this old mindset to create a new social system.

Governments have been tossed around by the technological storms with no ideological compass to guide them. Their response has been largely to get out of the way. Deregulation in the economic spheres of life has followed as perceived governmental helplessness has been transmuted into a new dogma of individual self-reliance.

Technology

Smart companies working at the leading edge of change are developing a new system of working. For example, 3Com, a computer networking business with headquarters in Santa Clara in the USA, is based on self-organizing work teams. Nobody at 3Com is contracted to work a set number of hours. These teams arrange round-the-clock working and determine their own schedules. It means that before a team in the USA finishes work it might pass a project over to another in India, which continues the work while their American colleagues sleep. The Indian team would then pass the project back the next day so that development is continuous. Another team may prefer to organize its work in twelve-hour rotating shifts.

Journalists working on an audio business programme, *Business Essentials*, which is distributed to subscribers on cassettes, collect their material in the UK and then send it down the telephone for editing in Australia. In this way, material can be edited during the British night and be back in London for the following day.

In similar but different vein, the old idea of the sleeping continent has been resurrected. The sleeping continent was a phenomenon in telecommunications whereby telephone traffic would be routed through the continent that was asleep. So it was often easier to route calls across the Atlantic eastwards via Russia and the Far East. Now, American insurance companies send claim forms to the west of Ireland for processing so that when the US company starts work again the next day the processed forms have been transmitted back from Ireland.

It is all a far cry from a generation ago when an international telephone call had to be booked in advance. Improved capability and decreased cost has led to the ubiquity of the new communications technologies. They allow us to manipulate time as a matter of course. Email shifts time, as do the answerphone and the fax, allowing messages to be sent, stored and retrieved later. Combined with the ability of instant transmission to shrink time, technology has made the idea of the fixed 9 to 5 working day redundant for many people. There is no need to know when someone will be somewhere in order to contact them and vice versa. Messages can be left in the great pigeon-hole in cyberspace. Work follows the person and takes place in the many different locations in which individuals find themselves.

The falling cost of electronic communications has made it economic to organize work on a round-the-clock global basis. A transatlantic telephone call in 1999 costs less than 1.5 per cent of what it cost in 1939. By 2010 the cost will probably be down to less than 1p a minute. A single transistor that cost $70 in the mid-1960s is now virtually free at a millionth of a cent.

Another effect of the new technologies is disintermediation. Intermediaries in many industries do little more than collect information. Estate agents hold a list of properties for sale, travel agents know which airlines are flying where at what times and at what prices, stockbrokers place orders for their clients at the best price through an exchange. All these agents are vulnerable to on-line technologies such as public, open internets and private, closed intranets. A global spot market is instantly available through such a system and enables anyone who is connected to the particular system to buy and sell any time they choose.

While the prospects of this technology are liberating to customers, the speed of the change is breath-taking and potentially damaging to producers. As nearly all of us are at one moment acting as a consumer and the next as a producer it is not surprising that there is an ambivalence to the changes. They are happening so fast there is no time to work out the new social structures that are needed to cope with them. Insecurity in the workplace and the home have raised issues of self-identity, relationships as well as money and status. The need to work hard and be seen to be successful is a source of the time pressure that is so predominant today.

Technology is often wrongly accused of destroying jobs. Closing a shipyard is highly visible, whereas opening new, small software companies is not. Yet over 10 million people world-wide now work in software. The gales of destruction caused by technology are more akin to the natural fires that destroy parts of a forest. When the ashes have cooled, new, vigorous growth advances quickly.

With the technological revolution much has been made of the end of work.[1] But in its 1996/97 *World Employment Report*, the International Labour Office (ILO) found no global evidence to support this. It states:

> while there has been some increase in self-employment, part-time work and other non-standard forms of employment, this has not meant the

disappearance of regular jobs. Data on job tenure do not show any gener-
alised decline in either the period employed individuals have been with
their current employer or projected future tenure. At the same time there
is also no evidence that the rate of job change has increased in labour
markets.[2]

Of course, none of this is meant to argue that the world of work is won-
drously pleasant or secure. It rarely is. But for all the centuries of its history,
capitalism has drawn an ever-larger share of the population into paid labour,
while never supplying as many jobs as people would like. In other words,
unemployment is a constant feature of economic life, rising in bad times and
falling in good. There has been no long-term structural change in the relationship between economic growth and employment growth. In areas of high
unemployment in some parts of Europe, the main causes are slow growth and
economic collapse, respectively, not technological transformation.

But new technologies have created insecurities. Electronic communication has, in particular, contributed to the general angst by enabling incessance and intrusion to dominate our work lives. There is now no escape from
work. It may be apocryphal but a leading UK retail bank is said to insist that
its senior staff keep their mobile phones switched on permanently on pain of
disciplinary action. As a matter of course investment bankers give their
mobile numbers to whoever might need to contact them – and never switch
their phones off. Now 24 hour accessibility is demanded in many sectors.

Whereas it was once possible to gain an extra day for a reply to a customer
by claiming to have just missed the post it is simply not acceptable in the age
of the fax and email. 'Yesterday we were content to wait two weeks for an
answer to a letter. Today, someone who doesn't answer email within the hour
is an obstructionist.' [3]

The clear lines of demarcation that existed between the home and the
workplace have begun to dissolve in our electronically connected society. In
the film *Play it Again Sam* (1972), Woody Allen's homage to *Casablanca*
(1942), a running joke is the way in which the character played by Marshall
Brickman continually telephones his office from wherever he is, in the days
before the advent of mobile phones, to tell them his location and telephone
number. This incessant behaviour was considered unusual enough to be

funny in the mid-1970s. Now it has become the norm and it is reshaping the workplace.

This inter-connectivity will intensify as today's younger generations age. They have grown up with electronic communications. Teenagers now regard the telephone as an extension of themselves. They have no special telephone manner when they use the instrument. Nor are they as concerned about the evening watershed. People in their forties and over who may not have grown up with a ubiquitous telephone are still apprehensive about receiving telephone calls after 9 p.m. If the telephone rings after 10 p.m. then it must be a death in the family. Their teenage children have no such inhibitions.

This electronic culture restructures our way of living. A new fluidity is available as people can check and recheck arrangements and issues while on the move. Being able to telephone and say that you are going to be ten minutes later than planned, or could the meeting place be changed, may not sound like the epitome of freedom in both domestic and working life. But such simple changes shape living into an incessant flow rather than a succession of fixed points. Think back to life before the mobile phone. There were many spaces in the day to be private, for example in the car or on a train. Now, even airlines have installed satellite telephone services on international aircraft, which allow users to plug in their laptops and send faxes. Bulkhead phones are also available. Those discrete, private spaces and times have gone and are now filled with conversation. We are in the process of reversing the historical pattern of thousands of years that moved us from the very public lifestyle of the past into the very private lifestyle epitomized by the suburban semi-detached home.

This reversal will be facilitated as the technology continually improves. The mobile phone will eventually be reduced to an in-ear device that will also function as a radio transmitter operating in conjunction with a wrist microphone. Combine this with voice recognition software and it is possible to see how somebody could dictate emails that will be produced and dispatched while walking down the street. A transparent folding visor attached to a hat will provide a screen to view incoming information such as graphics and spreadsheets. If that sounds too futuristic, IBM has already demonstrated a mobile telephone with a small display screen that is easily readable using a built-in magnifying mirror.

A mobile phone, an electronic organizer and a seat at a café table constitute a new workplace. Work starts when the phone is switched on. This future reality is already on offer at Waterside, British Airways' new office complex near Heathrow. Built on 240 acres of reclaimed land, the £200 million facility was opened in July 1998. Instead of employees having individual offices and desks, the building is based on a covered central street containing a café, shops and exhibition areas, surrounded by six blocks of open plan offices. To save employees having to use their own personal time, other on-site shops include a bank, travel centre, fitness suite, hairdresser and beauty salon. Complementing the new thinking behind this building, Waitrose the supermarket has introduced a novel time-saving service. Staff at Waterside can order their groceries through their employer's electronic network. Payment is made on-screen through a charge card and the orders are delivered to the workplace later in the day.

Waterside is based on the portability of electronic technologies. Any place I plug my laptop is the office. The employee can, if necessary, remain in a fixed place, the home for example. One consequence is that the information moves, not the person. In this light, the growth of tele-working can be seen as another possible means of alleviating the time-stress crisis among employees by allowing them to save on commuting time and also organize their own day. Hyped for some years as the saviour of our over-stressed social system, tele-working has been disappointingly slow to take off. The Department for Education and Employment (DfEE) has two definitions for tele-workers, namely the wider definition encompassing those who work at least one day a week at home and use the home as a base for their work the other days; the narrow definition refers to people whose main job of work is mostly at home. There were just over 1 million tele-workers under the wide definition in autumn 1997 and 238,000 on the narrow definition.[4] Tele-working is likely to grow because of two factors: concern about the effect of work and commuting on employees, and the availability of low-cost hardware and software solutions.

Video-conferencing could be another time-saver, removing the need to travel. It has been available since the early 1970s but until now video-conferencing required dedicated facilities and has been a high-cost item. The development of increasingly powerful PCs, ISDN lines, video cameras and software mean that for little more than £1,500 it is possible to equip a home office that can transmit voice, text and video pictures. This presents the opportunity for a split working week, two days at home, three days at the office for instance. Such permutations are being actively explored by firms who see it not only as a way of offering employees the means to introduce more flexibility into their own lives but also as a means of reducing their own office space requirements. Facilities managers in the City of London, which has some of the highest-cost real estate on earth, are actively investigating these possibilities as a means of reducing their expensive office space requirements. If everyone works at home one day a week on a rotating basis, there is a 20 per cent reduction in required office space.

The idea behind Waterside and other new workplaces is that technology can help develop new and more collaborative working practices. If information is power then the theory goes that sharing information will produce a more democratic and accessible culture that will not be bound by the rigid time constraints of the 9 to 5 day. This will result in a more productive and relaxed workforce. Similar thinking is behind the commercial use of the Internet, only here the target is a more relaxed consumer.

The global nature of business has been increasing rapidly since the late 1980s but few innovations will have more impact than the Internet. The Internet's main attraction for non-tangible products is that ordering is virtually instantaneous. Holidays can be booked, car insurance bought, estate agents' lists viewed – from companies anywhere in the world, any time day or night, from home or work and all in the time it takes to make a few key strokes. As the technology improves, the speed of electronic transmission will bring about comprehensive home ordering. The human voice transmits at around 55 bits a second, current modems manage about 30,000 bits a second and optical fibre connections will transmit in gigabits, more than 1 billion bits a second. The entire Argos catalogue and those of other direct marketing organizations could be downloaded onto the PC in a matter of seconds. Smart agents can be instructed by the PC user to search these catalogues for a required product or service, a consumer database is then checked to establish how well the selected range performed on consumer tests and then the most appropriate item will be selected and ordered. As the number of Internet connections grows, our notions of what is local will change as we communicate constantly with places on the other side of the world.

Globalization

In 1994, when Bill Clinton proposed to tax futures and options trading in the hopes of dampening market volatility, Jack Sandner, a Chicago Mercantile Exchange official, warned the US President in a public statement that if he were to do so, business would move overseas in a nanosecond. Clinton caved in. Less than a year later, Royal Dutch Shell decided that in order to avoid paying UK National Insurance contributions for British sailors it would simply transfer their contracts to Singapore and administer them from the Isle of Man.[5]

What connects these two totally disparate stories is globalization. There is an intuitive understanding of what globalization means and with it an uneasy feeling about how much in control of events we really are or can be in a world of large, transnational organizations. Anthony Giddens defines it as 'the intensification of world-wide social relations which link distant localities in such a way that local happenings are shaped by events occurring many miles away and vice versa.'[6] While others may not be as precise, most appreciate that just as the dominant metaphor in chaos theory is the beating of the butterfly wing leading to a hurricane a thousand miles away, so the opening of McDonald's in Beijing somehow affects our lives on the other side of the world. We do not know how, but we are pretty sure that it does. Not many people know what a nanosecond is but they know what Sandner meant.

This is not to say that the conversation down the pub is all about an individual's identity crisis in a period of global change. But there is a general understanding of the erosion of borders and barriers and the new permeability of the world. By 1990, 40 per cent of IBM employees were non-Americans, nearly all of them living and working outside the USA, and General Electric was the biggest private sector employer in Singapore.

Globalization is more than just a new and larger economic system. In many respects there has been a global economy, at least among the western nations, for some 400 years. Pedants will say that international trade was high before the First World War. It is also true that most of the major transnational firms still operate as flag-planters in that they are controlled and owned predominantly in their home country and operate abroad as colonial powers. But the movement of capital around the world and the new geometry of production that is developing, in which firms take a global view of location, is an inexorable trend.

With little help from declining trade unions and governments in thrall to market solutions, employers are able to determine working conditions. Companies are able to use the phenomenon of globalization, whether real or imagined, as one stick to develop an aggressive workplace culture. Even if employees work regular hours there is a feeling of instability and that at any time their working conditions could be changed. Manufacturing industries in a just-in-time culture work to a rhythm that is established on a global scale, while service industries have to meet whatever local demand is placed on them. There are no 'Wait Here' signs in a global world. It is no wonder that as the rules of globalization are worked out, the individual feels anxious and pressured. Relieving that individual pressure through holidays and leisure has become a huge industry in its own right.

Tourism

Sometime in the 1980s tourism took over from oil as the world's largest industry. A quarter (26 per cent) of British adults took at least two holidays a year in 1994, quadruple the figure in 1964. The best estimates suggest that world tourism accounts for around 10 per cent of world gross national product (GNP). [7] Perhaps one in nine of the global workforce is employed in tourism. In the UK, the industry is worth about £35 billion a year. The world's largest industry is projected to grow by over 3 per cent a year between 1999 and 2009. In the process of becoming the dominant industry, tourism has affected the balance between the local and the global.

Tourist locations offer themselves on the basis of their local appeal. This can be the scenery, beaches, climate, culture, cuisine, heritage or a permutation of any of these and more. But their intensely local appeal is quickly traduced by the tourism industry. This is because we no longer live in a world where most people 'travel' but one which is structured for mass tourist consumption. Travellers do not interfere with the area they are visiting. They use the transport of the locals, sleep in their homes, eat their food. But to visit

41

and not have an impact can happen only if the number of travellers is small. Tourism is a mass activity. Tourists come to look and see but do so on their own terms. They maintain their own perception of time, not that of their hosts, in the same way as they eat their way through tourist menus rather than taste the local cuisine. They reshape the area they are visiting and the behaviour of the locals to suit their needs.

Tourists operate on a seven day, 24 hour clock. They do not differentiate between the weekday and the weekend during the course of their holiday and they suspend their own local differentiation between night and day. For them, time is divided into a series of 'wants' to be served – I want to eat, I want to drink, I want to swim, I want to visit some sites, I want to dance and so on. It bears little relation to local time but if the local people want the global tourists then they must conform. They must be open when the tourists want them to be open. If it is All Saints Day in Florence, no matter. The exhibitions and art galleries are open as are the shops aimed at tourists. In the late 1970s this would not have been the case but the increasing economic importance of tourism has forced these changes.

When the Royal Academy of Arts in London previously put on a Monet exhibition, it attracted 658,000 visitors, of whom some 20 per cent were tourists. In 1999 the organizers hope that the Monet exhibition will attract 1 million people, and to accommodate the demands of the home visitors and the 200,000 or more expected tourists, the exhibition will be open until 10 p.m. on at least two evenings a week. Providing this flexibility in entry times is of vital importance to tourists, who seldom have the option to come back on another day. And if the art galleries, shops, heritage sites and the rest are to be open, then the people who work in them must be prepared to accept flexibility in their working hours.

Another example of tourist demand is the through-the-night, open-topped double decker bus 'hopper' sightseeing trips around London. They were begun by London Pride in July 1998 and were so successful that the company intends to make this a regular feature of the summer months. This through-the-night city tour is a world first and the company says that it meets the demands of tourists who do not accept being told that something is closed.

In the near future, visitors to the UK may be able to get a drink when they want rather than having to deal with the British licensing laws. This is one aspect of deregulation, the catch-all governmental response to many of the new forces reshaping the world.

Deregulation

It is not necessary to be a raving right-wing libertarian to realize we live in a paternalistic society. Given half a yard, any authority will take a mile in exerting social control over a population. The powers that be in the western world have long tried to use regulation to decree how large parts of society spends their time. Soon after mechanical clocks first appeared, the authorities realized that it gave them a new means of ordering the lives of citizens. In 1391, not long after the appearance of a clock in the town square made the idea of reasonably accurate hourly times practicable, there was a town decree in Cologne that any foreigner in the city with a safe conduct should be off the streets by 9 p.m. (by 8 p.m. in winter). The curfew was applied to armed people in the beginning of 1398 and by the end of that year there was a general curfew that after 11 p.m. 'no priest, no student, no layman, no woman and no man' should be on the streets.[8]

In a laudable attempt at self-abnegation, in the UK in September 1997 the Labour government established the Better Regulation Task Force. This quango has sensibly recognized that any regulation must have broad public support. The Task Force points out that the public's view can change over time and what is acceptable regulation at one time will not be so to another generation and vice versa. For instance, drink-driving laws, which were largely ineffective for many years, are now working well. Sunday shopping restrictions, on the other hand, which had been well respected for over a century, suddenly lost credibility as it was recognized that it was possible to buy pornography but not a bible on a Sunday. The restrictions were widely and illegally ignored and eventually drastically reduced. To be accepted, according to the Task Force, regulation also has to be enforceable, easy to understand, balanced and thought out.

Similar thinking in the previous Conservative administration lay behind the decision in December 1994 to introduce new Home Office regulations that enabled shops to open 24 hours a day Monday to Saturday. Until then, and despite the unsuccessful efforts at reform by Mrs Thatcher while Prime

Minister, the Shops Act 1950 meant that most shops had to close at 8 p.m. with the option to stay open until 9 p.m. on one night a week. Sunday trading in larger stores was still confined to six hours in total under the terms of the Sunday Trading Bill passed in November 1993, while unrestricted opening was allowed to smaller stores.

In other EU countries there has been similar deregulation of what has often been little more than vested interest masquerading as principle. When the Bundestag Lower House voted in June 1996 to allow evening shopping hours to be extended from 6.30 p.m. to 8 p.m. during the week and from 2 p.m. to 4 p.m. on Saturdays, it was voting on the side of consumers against those shopkeepers who had wanted protection from larger and more efficient competitors. The protectionist culture had been enshrined in a 1956 law created specifically to prevent small stores from facing closure. It had made shopping something of a nightmare for millions of Germans who left work at 6 p.m. and then had to rush to the grocery, baker, pharmacist and department stores.

In the UK, broad public support for change is leading to the licensing laws restricting the sale of alcohol to be rethought. In keeping with the spirit that regulation must have broad public support, the Task Force seems to have decided that the licensing of the sale of alcohol needs to be liberalized.

Licensing has been part of a long, usually undeclared, war between the people and the government as to what is in whose best interest. Pub licensing hours were introduced in the First World War when Lloyd George, the Prime Minister and the least likely candidate to be regarded as a pillar of moral rectitude, proclaimed 'We are fighting Germany, Austria, and the drink.'[9] Initially, the restrictions on the hours of pub opening were confined to harbour areas and the armed forces. Then they were extended to workers in strategic industries such as munitions and finally to the general population.

Mainland Europe did not go in for such controls, which is one reason why the evening entertainment economy in so many European towns, based on eating and drinking, is so admired by the British. However, British towns are now emulating the rest of Europe as they declare themselves 24 hour cities. When the licensing restrictions are relaxed, Britain will have caught up with Reykjavik in Iceland, which allows opening until 1 a.m. in summer. In winter nobody in their right mind would be out of doors at that time anyway.

It is difficult to imagine that there will be any reversal of the deep structural factors that are reshaping the social world. Combined with the cultural shift from thrift to consumption we are irrevocably moving towards an ever more open and extended hours society.

4 So much to buy; so much to do; so little time to do it – how we became insatiable consumers and ended up choosing money over time

The car, the furniture, the wife, the children – everything has to be disposable. Because you see the main thing today is – shopping. Years ago a person, he was unhappy, didn't know what to do with himself – he'd go to church, start a revolution – something. Today, you're unhappy? Can't figure it out? What is the salvation? Go shopping.

Arthur Miller, *The Price*, Act II

For many of us there are not enough hours in the day. Not enough time to do all the things we want. There are two easy ways to solve the problem and one harder way. First, we could stop watching television. This would free up three to four hours a day. Easy. Second, we could stop buying so many goods and more especially services. Easy again. This would save some time and solve the problem. We would not need shops opening round the clock. Three or four hours a day would do – like they used to in Poland.

Third, if we purchased less we would not need to earn as much and so we could work fewer hours. This would be going some of the way to a more sustainable society, with less packaging, less pollution, less of everything.

We could do all these things but there is about the same chance of it happening as there is of pigs flying. To understand why we cannot reduce our consumption as easily as all that, we have to have some understanding of human behaviour and why it is that we have become consuming animals.

Needs and wants

Insatiable wants and their satisfaction have been one of the cornerstones of economic theory for over a century. Alfred Marshall, one of the founders of economics, wrote, 'human wants and desires are countless in number and various in kind.'[1] Turn to consumption in an economics textbook and you will find something along the lines of 'Human wants and desires are infinite but resources are limited'. That is the basic economic problem.

While there may be much to mock in the basic tenets of the rational, utility-maximizing individuals of economic literature on the question of wants the economists were right: they are limitless. Non-economists are disturbed by this, due to their confusion between wants and needs. To the economist a 'need' is something that is in a real sense beyond price. We have an absolute need for oxygen and water. We need a certain number of calories a day containing essential nutrients. We also need warmth and shelter. Reproduction is not a need as such for humans, no matter what evolutionary psychologists say about 'selfish' genes,[2] but unless the individual reproduces in one way or another we shall soon end up like the celibate Shakers, possessing beautiful kitchens but with few people left to enjoy them.

The range of price-insensitive needs is limited. It is no different from any other animal and for much of human history it has been the miserable lot of many to live not much better than animals. It is our emotional and socialized wants and desires, embedded in the process of consumption, that are limitless.

> Consumers may purchase ready-made meals, travel on packaged tours, watch sports on television or listen to music on radio or discs, or drive a car they must not attempt to repair themselves. Modern consumers are physically passive but mentally they are very busy. Consumption is more than ever before an experience which is to be located in the head, a matter of the brain and mind, rather than seen as the process of simply satisfying basic biological needs.[3]

We have now learned to consume so well that at the end of the twentieth century, we no longer simply want, but 'want to want under all circumstances and at all times irrespective of what goods and services are actually required or consumed.'[4] The huge shopping malls around Britain each attract more visitors in a year than the Vatican does tourists.

The idea that we have become consuming machines with insatiable wants is hard for many people to swallow. It goes against the Puritan instinct, makes a mockery of environmentalism and seems morally improper. Insatiable consumption suggests waste and unthinking profligacy. We still feel a frisson of moral outrage when we read that a glitterati couple spent £750 on champagne to fill a hotel bath,[5] or that Sir Elton John can get through a quarter of a million pounds a week on his credit card. Yet it would be wrong to throw stones as it seems we spend nearly 10 per cent of our time just gathering information about products and services. There are twenty-three different magazines on regular sale in Britain about homes and interiors; there are fourteen on fishing, seven on hair and fourteen general motoring magazines. On top of that are supplements, free sheets, lifestyle magazines and wall-to-wall TV programmes.

To understand why we are reluctant to trade money for time, why we will not down-shift to a simpler and less consumer-orientated way of life as a way of solving the time-squeeze, we need an understanding of consumption and its history.

Turning wants into needs

Our great-great-great grandparents did not go out and shop. Consumption is not the natural order of things. While the elite have, throughout history, been able to enjoy luxury in both goods and services, the lot of the common man and woman has been little better than subsistence. Just as the industrial society, the other major transformation of the past two centuries, had to be created so too a consumer society had to be constructed. Our forebears had to start learning to want.

Until the middle of the nineteenth century there was still a close connection between production and consumption. Craft workers usually knew the consumer of their goods, idealized in the small farming communities in the USA. This society, which produced the likes of Henry Ford and the other founders of the era of industrial and consumer expansion, was based on a religiously inspired work-ethic, thrift and a sturdy individualism. Consumption as we would know it was self-regulated, reserved for special events such as religious festivals and infrequent carnivals.

In this way of thinking, most goods were wholly functional; they had a value in use, as Marx put it. A chair, for example, was made to last and would be thrown out only when it was beyond repair. To move into the modern world of complete consumption required the overthrow of the dominance of frugality. In 1947 this was articulated in the USA as:

> The major problem confronting us is how to move this merchandise to the American consumer. The major problem therefore is one of stimulating the urge to buy!... Our willingness to part with something before it is completely worn out is... truly an American habit and it is soundly based on our economy of abundance. It must be further nurtured even though it is contrary to one of the oldest inbred laws of humanity – the law of thrift – of providing for the unknown and often-feared day of scarcity.'6

The twentieth century's triumph of marketing and advertising has been overcoming the law of thrift by translating wants into needs. The opening lines of a 1998 advertisement for a travel company demonstrates this: 'Picture this, five minutes ago you left the calm of your hotel and now you're among the bustle on Florence's Ponte Vecchio. Of the small jewellery shops that crowd the ancient bridge we'd point you towards Gherardi's. Inside you'll find a veritable treasure trove, which may well tempt you into buying something you never knew you needed.'7 A want is transferred into a purchase and is justified on the basis that it is now a need. 'I need this and I deserve it' has become one of the slogans of our age.

The poet Philip Larkin pinned down the start of sexual intercourse to 1963. It's harder to say when consumption as such began. One school of thought dates the start of the move to the late sixteenth century at the court of Elizabeth I of England. Another believes it was a hundred years later with the influx of cheap dyed cotton from India.8 A reasonable case can be made for the beginning of middle-class consumption starting in the middle part of the eighteenth century. This generation, the grandsons and granddaughters of the Puritans, benefited from their forebears' parsimony. Kick-starting economic growth requires an initial generation to be hard-working and thrifty so that it can invest. The ascetic lifestyles of the Puritans ideally fitted them for the role, a lesson that Gordon Brown as UK Chancellor of the Exchequer seems to have taken to heart. The Puritans' grandchildren, however, were cut from a far less severe cloth.

Throughout the eighteenth century Britain prospered and consumerism began to spread through the social classes. Neil McKendrick, a major writer on the growth of consumption, has shown how important a period it was:

> What men and women had once hoped to inherit from their parents they now expected to buy for themselves. What were once bought at the dictate of need were now bought at the dictate of fashion. What were once bought for life might now be bought several times over. What were once available only on high days and holidays through the agency of markets were increasingly made available every day except Sunday through the additional agency of an ever-advancing network of shops and shopkeepers. As a result luxuries came to be seen as mere 'decencies' and 'decencies' came to be seen as 'necessities'.[9]

During this period many techniques of modern marketing were introduced by Josiah Wedgwood, who recognized the importance of the opinion-leader in the hierarchical, class-bound society of the time. The strategy was simple. He targeted the upper classes, often with complimentary loans of tableware, believing that by setting a style the goods would then trickle down to the middle and lower classes. It was an early example of what we might now call 'celebrity endorsement'.

By introducing new lines Wedgwood also developed the notion of fashion. Goods began to be valued for their style. As styles changed, the idea of repeat purchases was introduced, requiring goods to be bought over and over again to keep up with fashion. Consequently, the consumer had to spend more time on consumption and learn to judge not only the fashionable from the unfashionable but also what other messages were contained within the purchase.

While the middle classes were prospering in the eighteenth century, life for the vast bulk of the population was stupendously hard. Working hours were still horrendous. In 1776, Paris bookbinders went on strike for a reduction to a fourteen-hour day.[10] A poor diet, scant possessions and non-existent savings left little possibility for consumption among the urban and rural masses. In such a near-subsistence society wants were simple and for the most part satisfied by the church on the one hand and the gin palace on the other.

Although mass consumption as we know it did not begin in earnest for another 180 years, the nineteenth century was one of increasing involvement in consumption by the working class. However, by the end of the century most working people were still too poor to afford more than a few items over and above the staples of life.

Cometh the hour, cometh the man in the shape of Henry Ford, who, unwittingly, was to do more than any other to bring about the modern age of consumption. Ford was typical of the skilled working men of his time. Born in Dearborn, Michigan, in 1863, at 16 he walked to Detroit and apprenticed himself to a mechanic for $2.50 a week. His board was $3.50, so he worked four hours every night for a watchmaker for $2 a week.

Ford did not understand the modern notion of consumption of wanting to want. It was not simply because as a young man he had only $1 a week to spend, it just was not part of his background. He came from a society where goods were made to be used and to last. To him a car was just another tool, like a tractor. When he said of the Model T, 'Any colour, as long as it is black', it was because it was inconceivable to him, with his Protestant, farming background, that the colour could possibly matter. Anyway, black was the cheapest paint around.

But he did understand the working person's aspiration for a better life. Ford wrote the best example of what today would be called the company vision or mission statement:

> I will build a motor car for the great multitude. It will be constructed of the best materials, by the best men and women to be hired, after the simplest designs that modern engineering can devise. Any person making a good salary will be able to own one. And enjoy with his family the blessings of hours of pleasure. In God's great open spaces.[11]

It is a powerful, instrumental vision and contains the seeds of the consumer revolution of the twentieth century. Ford may not have understood the cultural nature of modern consumption but he realized that the increased productivity that came from his automated techniques would create an over-supply of goods unless there was equivalent demand. He linked production to consumption and in so doing inaugurated the consumer age in which we live.

In 1900, the German motor company Daimler-Benz was predicting total European demand for cars at fewer than 1,500, the number of families the company estimated would be able to afford a chauffeur. At the time, virtually no American families owned a car. In 1910 only 1 per cent did. As Ford began using standardized interchangeable parts and assembly-line techniques in his plant in 1913, the rate of productivity leapt. By 1920 26 per cent of US families had at least one car. This democratization of ownership came about as a result of rising productivity and Ford's other great contribution, the $5 day.

Although Ford was not the first to employ such practices, he was chiefly responsible for the general adoption of the assembly line to mass production and for the consequent great expansion of American industry.

By early 1914 this innovation, although greatly increasing productivity, had resulted in a monthly labour turnover of 40–60 per cent in his factory, largely because of the unpleasant monotony of assembly-line work and repeated increases in the production quotas assigned to workers. Ford met this difficulty by doubling the daily wage then standard in the industry, raising it from about $2.50 to $5. The net result was increased stability in his labour force and a substantial reduction in operating costs.

The increased pay was not a humanitarian gesture. It was part of a process of social control that produced an industrial system known as Fordism. It started the move to modern consumption. Ford understood not only that, 'If you cut wages you just cut the number of your customers', but also the obverse, if you raise wages you create customers.[12] By paying his workers they would be able to afford the cars they were making.

But that alone does not explain how the culture of thrift was dealt with. How to get people to spend rather than save.

The rise of advertising

Astute business people recognize that increasing demand is not just a question of money. The Boston department store owner, Edward A. Filene, said in 1919: 'mass production demands the education of the masses; the masses must learn to behave like human beings in a mass production world... They must achieve not mere literacy, but culture.'[13] The mass production of commodities in ever-increasing abundance demands a mass market to absorb them.[14] This was clearly stated by the US President's Committee on Recent Economic Changes that reported in 1929: 'wants are almost insatiable; that one want satisfied makes way for another. By advertising and other promotional devices, by scientific fact-finding, and by carefully predeveloped consumption, a measurable pull on production was created.'[15]

But not measurable enough. By the early 1930s this was a serious issue as markets collapsed in the wake of the the 1929 stockmarket crash and drop in demand. Although those in work were still earning and as a result of price decreases were in fact increasingly better off, there was a reluctance to spend.

An American advertising man, Earnest Elmo Calkins, had come up with the solution in 1927 that was the next step on the way to the new consumerism. He wrote:

> Goods fall into two classes, those we use, such as motor-cars or safety razors, and those we use up, such as toothpaste or soda biscuit. Consumer engineering must see to it that we use up the kind of goods we now merely use. Would any change in the goods or habits of people speed up their consumption? Can they be displaced by newer models? Can artificial obsolescence be created? Consumer engineering does not end until we can consume all we can make.[16]

Calkins introduced the idea of designing obsolescence into the product itself as a way of stimulating consumption. The industrial designers and marketing men and women were so successful at this that in the USA General Motors (GM) design chief Harley Earl was able to claim in 1955 that in 1934 'average car ownership span was five years; now it is two years. When it is one year we will have a perfect score.'

Tentative steps along the same path in Britain were stymied by the Second World War but the long post-war boom that lasted until the 1973 oil crisis was the perfect economic backdrop to overthrow the thrift culture and institute the new consumerism. Gross domestic product (GDP) in Britain grew by 30 per cent in the 1950s and by the end of the decade rationing had become a folk memory. The nascent consumerism that had begun to develop before the war returned. As incomes rose, the Prime Minister Harold Macmillan was able to claim in 1957 that most of the people had never had it so good and win the 1959 general election on the back of it.

The increasing prosperity began to be translated into material goods. By the early 1960s 80 per cent of homes in Britain had hot running water, 50 per cent had a washing machine, over 70 per cent had a television and over 30 per cent had at least one car. The advertising profession realized, far sooner than the academics, that a seminal shift was underway. While the sociologists were still arguing about production as the dominant mode in a capitalist society, market researchers, advertisers, media owners and retailers were forging a new understanding of the consumer. In the spirit of Calkins they realized the malleability of a customer who was susceptible to a new way of doing things.

Restrictions on borrowing were reduced as first hire-purchase regulations were relaxed and then overall credit restrictions.

> The banks... changed their position in relation to their client groups, shifting responsibility onto the ordinary person, moving from a discourse of duty to one of choice. Before the era of the credit card, if someone wanted to borrow in an agreed way, they had to apply to the bank for a loan in person, and legislation dictated that for durable goods the purchaser had to put down a proportion of the price before they could be given a loan. The credit card changed this: the client is free to spend the allowed credit wherever and whenever they choose.[17]

Independent television was introduced in Britain in 1956 but it was still a black and white world. With the lack of colourfast materials, clothing was drab, cinema films were often in monochrome and there was little colour in the magazines. That changed as a result of improvements in printing technology on the one hand and the media owners' realization that a growing section of the population had money to spend. On 4 February 1962 the first *Sunday Times* colour magazine was published. The cover featured eleven pictures of the model Jean Shrimpton taken by David Bailey. It could well be argued that this was when modern mass consumption in the UK was born. Eighteen months later the *Observer* and the *Sunday Telegraph* followed suit. By 1965 the *Sunday Times* was regularly featuring food, fashion, travel, the arts and home furnishing in its editorial. New standards in design and photography transferred consumption from wanting things for themselves to wanting them to define who you were. It was the start of lifestyle marketing. In the ten heady years of the 1960s GDP rose by 40 per cent and people had begun to learn to want to want.[18] The new age of consumerism had begun.

The meaning of modern consumerism

French academic Jean Baudrillard, one of the most 'difficult' of modern sociologists, strongly argued that the media are the formative influence in creating a new culture of consumption. He suggested that over the past 200 years we have not changed in any biological sense, evolution does not work that fast. If what we perceive as needs today are vastly more complex than they would have been in the past then it is because of expansion not evolution. Baudrillard's answer as to where these expanded needs came from was marketing and advertising, particularly in the past few decades.[19]

In Baudrillard's world there is no such thing as objective events that are then reported on by an external media. The media and the event are synonymous, the one doesn't occur without the other. Politics becomes the soundbite, sports events take place at times to suit the TV channels, and the sinking of the *Titanic* is a film, a CD and T-shirt, a consumption experience. What is seen is what is. In this world it is not truth that matters but media credibility.

In such a hyper-real world, where reality and its simulation blend into one, there is a free-floating landscape of signs such as Coca Cola, Calvin Klein, Tesco, Virgin, Dunhill and Sainsbury, that are attached and detached to products at will. In the new consumer society we consume not so much the products themselves but the signs. Brewers talk of their customers as 'drinking the advertising'. There are advertisements for beers and lagers that use stylized and constructed Irish national identities as the emotional attachment for the product. Advertisements for tourism in Scotland are equally romantic. If the products attached to the advertising were to be transposed, few would notice the difference. It is the signs that we consume, the desires and wants that we have, rather than the products themselves that are of consequence. We can run into a satiation problem with products – we can literally eat only so much – but there is virtually no end to our wanting of signs. In this sense we do have insatiable wants, we can never stop wanting to want.

Charles Revson, the founder of the Revlon cosmetics firm, is supposed to have said, 'In the factory we manufacture cosmetics, in the shop we sell hope.' Even the lonely Eleanor Rigby kept her face in a jar by the door. It does not require too much analysis to accept that a large number of goods have a meaning way beyond their functional value. Cosmetics and perfumes, Rolex watches, Mont Blanc pens, red roses, Armani suits – all come laden with universal and individual meanings about status, aspiration, economic success, the so-called lifestyle statements. The meaning can come from within the product itself – turkey with the trimmings equals Christmas and all the images that thought evokes. Or it can come from the brand associated with the product – Nike, Coca Cola, Virgin. Meaning also depends on context. A black executive car and a mobile phone can mean a company executive or drug dealer depending on where and when.

Today we are defined more by the way we live and what we own than by what we do.

> Earlier, value was added in production. Marketing then focussed on purchase. Value is now added in consumption. Personal identity is created and recreated on the basis of usage rather than on the basis of production or purchase. Many people identify and communicate themselves by their consumption activities, their sports, hobbies or music preferences rather than their jobs.[20]

We both enjoy our possessions and are entrapped by them. All this is understood by the people who produce advertising, design shop interiors, make promotional videos, plan media campaigns, conduct focus groups and do all the other things that make up the marketing industry. They have been largely responsible for embedding meaning into the goods and services they promote. And the consumers enter into consensual compliance – they want to consume and enjoy consuming. After watching TV, shopping is the most popular leisure pursuit.

We have moved on from Max Weber's description of the ethic of capitalism as one of self-denial to one that is all about self-gratification. Pierre Bourdieu, a French sociologist, has suggested a new approach to pleasure. The old bourgeoisie, he argues, based its life on a morality of duty, where a combination of reserve, modesty and restraint made them associate every satisfaction of forbidden impulses with guilt. In contrast, the new middle class urges pleasure as a duty. This doctrine makes it a failure, a threat to self-esteem, not to have fun.[21] Pleasure is seen not only as a right but also as a responsibility.

It is easy to go overboard on this and most of the sociological literature does. Humans are largely creatures of contingent habit. People may have a favourite breakfast cereal but if there is none left in the cupboard, most people will eat whatever is around without considering that in some way it has irrevocably compromised their chosen lifestyles. It would be asking too much of people to continually adhere to some self-selected lifestyle. One of the problems of modern living that causes no end of anxiety is the incessant choice it presents.[22] When we have settled on a particular brand or supplier, we may well stay with that particular brand, even if the meaning associated with that brand changes over time. In the end people generally stick with what they know, simply because experimentation is too much trouble. When the alarm goes you get up – that's life.

Consuming from an early age

In the late 1990s, 50-year olds are the baby-boomer generation. When they were born at the end of the Second World War, time was not a problem for most children as there was so little competition for it. Most children played in the street or park nearby, a willing mother provided meals at set times, cinema clubs showed films on a Saturday mornings, *Journey into Space* was broadcast on radio and the only other major claims on children's time were school, the scouts and guides.

A youngster today is faced with huge time-management problems. There are school commitments, TV soaps, new CDs, videos, endless radio stations, computer games, music lessons and ballet classes. Play is no longer contained within the street. For many children playing a game of football usually requires dressing in the replica strip, finding an acquiescent adult to chauffeur them to the pitch, and taking a shower after the game – as dirt is an abomination to many of today's parents. What was once an hour's kick-about has become a three-hour saga.

The children of the baby-boomers have grown up in a media-rich, consumer-dominated environment. In the mid-1960s, a large survey of American students found that less than 50 per cent considered financial well-being as either essential or very important. Over the years, that has climbed to nearly 75 per cent.

Of course, in the 1960s it was easier for students to be somewhat more blasé about making money. Jobs were like buses: if you didn't get one, another would be along shortly. Their children who are now students have grown up in a world where business values have been fêted. In Britain a successful company career is becoming a requirement for entry into the portals of political power.

Companies exist essentially to make profits by providing end-users with products and services that are consumed. As consumption has become the dominant social mode so business has become the dominant organizational form, transcending Parliament, the courts, and other loci of power. If the purpose of living is to consume then it should be no surprise if today's younger generation view the world through that lens. It is the baby-boomers' legacy.

Today's teenagers are shaping their own style of consumption. To see the fallout of incessant choice, watch teenagers viewing television, continually flicking from station to station. It irritates their parents partly because age lessens the ability to hold different thoughts and experiences in our heads at the same time and so they cannot empathize with their children's actions, but mainly because they simply cannot see the need. Why can't kids watch one programme for at least a few minutes?

For a teenage generation who grew up with colour television, stereo hi-fi sound, videos and satellite dishes, the media are always in the background as part of their lives. Teenagers zap not because they have low attention spans. When it suits them they can concentrate as hard as anyone. They have purely constructed a different world from adults and consume it differently.

In many ways they are the first generation to have broken out of the rigid classificatory way of thinking. Today's teenagers live in a world of ambiguity where you can watch TV while not watching it *at the same time*. They are the first fuzzy consumers, to borrow a terminology from fuzzy logic.[23] What they cannot do is wait. The idea of delayed gratification and the other totems of the middle classes are meaningless to a generation that has never had to wait. They have grown up in a world of electronic products in which the product life cycle has been reduced to ninety days. The idea that a shop might be closed when they want to buy is a personal affront. For them a 24 hour world will seem as natural as it is alien to their grandparents.

Teenagers and young adults have been labelled generation X and operate on what has been called realtime.[24] They do what they need to do when they want to do it. Any harassed parent of children in their late teens and early twenties knows the mantra 'It's under control' which is the stock answer in any situation. Likewise, parents know that in most instances it is futile to fight their children's attitude. Some companies are beginning to learn this as well. Providing their younger workforce in particular with 24 hour access to a safe working environment, and turning something of a blind eye to their use of office equipment for personal activities such as telephoning friends at all hours of the day and night, is difficult for strait-laced company office managers to accept. But the smarter ones are doing just that.

We should not be surprised by our children. We have become insatiable and dissonant consumers. The one thing we will not do is solve the conundrum by the obvious means – reduce consumption whether that be of television, shopping, work or whatever. The same respondents who said in one survey that they did not have enough time, refused, in the main, to consider spending money to save time.

As consumers we have come a long way since the mid-1960s let alone since the 1790s. It required two driving factors. First, there had to be the vast growth in productivity that allowed people to have the income to enable them to choose. Technology gave the impetus for this increase in productivity and also made a vast qualitative difference to people's lives. Second, there was a change in social attitudes which meant consumption became an end in itself.

It is difficult to believe that there will be any slackening of these driving factors in the twenty-first century. If anything, it is a reasonable bet that they will intensify. We have learned to become consumers. We are all consumers now. We are unwilling to reduce our consumption in order to free up more time. The alternative is for us to rethink how we manage the time we have.

5 A very brief history of the meaning of time

I have been on a calendar but never on time.

Marilyn Monroe

Western societies have a real problem with time. Deep in the western psyche is the notion of life as a portion of time, the allotted biblical span of three score years and ten, which we have to make the most of in some self-fulfilling and purposive manner. Time is precious. It cannot be stored and banked like other commodities. It must be used wisely. As children we are taught not to waste time, time is money and procrastination is the thief of time. The Benedictine rule that 'idleness is the enemy of the soul' and the Puritan ethic of hard work and 'time well spent' were implicit in British public schooling. We are so obsessed with time that time management is now a growth industry and time managers teach good time-use habits to company executives all over the UK.

The materialist view of time causes difficulties. Our poor understanding of what time is and how it is constructed prevents us from having a better relationship with it. The 24 Hour Society offers a temporal rearrangement of our lives that will enable us to regain control. But as long as we are unsure about time we will see the 24 Hour Society as a threat rather than a benefit.

The meaning of time

We can measure time with amazing accuracy. An atomic clock set running 100 million years ago when dinosaurs tramped the earth would be correct today to within a second or two.[1] Time itself eludes precise definition. A leading British sociologist of time quoted an interviewee:

We talk about closing-time, lunch-time, getting-up time, and that time is up. What time is, that is more difficult to say. It is not a person, not a thing, not a vegetable. It's a period and units, the day chopped up into hours, minutes and seconds. But it also divides the past from the future. We can see the past in pictures and writing but we can't be there – that is *a* time. *The* time is now, this very second. But I do not know what we are chopping up into units. I think it's an illusion since there isn't anything to chop up.[2]

Physicists and philosophers have struggled with the nature of time. Stephen Hawking wrote a best-selling book on time and the universe.[3] The philosopher, John McTaggart, in the early twentieth century, developed a novel thesis about time that flew in the face of common sense. He asserted that time is unreal and does not exist. Despite the efforts of some of the best philosophical brains including Bertrand Russell and Michael Dummett, no definitive refutation of McTaggart's self-admittedly crazy idea has been produced.

Our perception of time is often influenced by our emotions. It really does seem to go faster when you are having fun. Albert Einstein, something of a male chauvinist, described its relativity as, 'When you sit talking to a nice girl for two hours it seems like two minutes; when you sit on a hot-stove for two minutes it seems like two hours.' He famously showed from his relativity equations that the closer an object approached the speed of light, the slower time passed compared to that of an observer. This time-dilation effect leads to the famous prediction, used in the film *Planet of the Apes* (1967), that if a spaceship left earth and travelled at close to the speed of light for a year, then on its return the voyagers would have aged a year but their earth-bound contemporaries would have been dead for many millennia.

There is no river of time in which we swim, it is a social construct that we create. We live in a society that regulates behaviour by explicit rules of legality and illegality and implicit rules that can be termed appropriate behaviour. What we can and cannot do are largely governed by the social censorship that says this is appropriate or not. These social conventions determine where and when we do things and themselves change over time. 'White dinner jackets are only worn East of Suez' describes not only ideas of space in the former British Empire but also a whole social system that has been out-dated. 'Early to bed and early to rise keeps a man healthy, wealthy and wise' was taught to generations of Britons as the way of organizing their time appropriately. To behave otherwise could lead to someone being labelled as difficult, lazy, eccentric or even worse.

In Britain society is governed by 'clock time'. Many people eat at 6.30 p.m. because that is supper-time. Other countries see time in a different perspective. In the more hedonistic culture of the Mediterranean and Latin America, time is secondary to enjoyment. People eat at 8, 9 or 10 p.m. when they are hungry and take more pleasure and time over the meal. In these societies, natural or 'event time' is the dominant construct. If we are going to find solutions to the time problem, the dualism between two types of time, event time and clock time, needs to be resolved into a new form of social time.

Event time

All humans are born with a sense of event time. Babies function in event time. They know when they are hungry or tired and want to eat or sleep when their bodies tell them. They are totally in touch with their internal needs. But from a young age they are trained to sleep and feed at set times. The baby learns when to be hungry and when to be sleepy. In research on obesity, it has been suggested that fat people eat in time with the clock, normal weight people respond to internal hunger pangs.[4]

When Diana, Princess of Wales, died in 1997, Britain entered what can be described as event or natural time. The clocks, metaphorically speaking, stopped. The normal cues given by the clock, which usually guided British lives, were ignored. Instead of taking direction from the structured world of clock time, people reverted to an earlier form of time-detached living that relied on listening to the body's physical and emotional needs. During that remarkable week between her death and her funeral, millions of Britons disrupted their normal schedules in ways they would otherwise do only in the case of a family bereavement or serious domestic issue. They queued for hours to sign books of condolence, laid flowers at the palaces in London and continued to suspend time until Sir Elton John pleaded it was time to move on. British commentators were shocked by the outpouring of emotion and the disregard of usual regularity. Many described the public displays of grief during the funeral as something that would have been expected in Italy or Spain, but not in Britain.

In event time, the world is seen through a different lens. Periods of time are related to natural events. Burmese monks know that it is time to get up, 'when it is light enough to see the veins in their hands'.[5] Muslims base it on the passage in the Quran that defines day-break as the time when it is possible to distinguish between a dark and a light thread. Farmyard life starts when the cock crows. As Robert Levine recounts in A Geography of Time, 'In parts of Madagascar, questions about how long something takes might receive the answer "the time of rice-cooking (about half an hour)" or "the frying of a locust (a quick moment)".' In the Andes, time is often measured by how long it takes to chew a quid of coca leaf; sometimes the destination is so many cigarettes away. The New English Dictionary used to contain the phrase 'pissing while', which may have depended on too large a number of variables to have any pretensions to accuracy but nevertheless has, as Levine says, 'a certain cross-cultural translatability'. [6]

Event time was the way in which the pre-industrial world lived. Imagine a world without clocks. What are the cues that give some sense of time? Each day we would see the sun rise and set. The moon rises and sets and waxes and wanes. The tides rise and fall. Seasons come and go and return again. Planets move across the sky and come back to their starting point. It is a world of endless cycles but essentially changeless. This does not mean that nothing changes because humans create not only artefacts but also a culture, but in its essentials life is very similar to that of our forebears.

This was the world of the Maya in Central America and many other peoples of the past. Time did not have a purposive direction and there was no notion of progress. Yet the Maya were literate and numerate. They could calculate the periodicity of the planet Venus with an accuracy of one part in 2 million, something that western astronomers were unable to do until over a thousand years later. The Maya had a very impressive calendar but they did not have a clock. They could not measure the continual passage of time.

This organic relationship to time results in a far more relaxed approach to punctuality and appointments. It is more important to see a friend of the family than to keep an appointment or to go to work. Mexicans, for example, are not too bothered about letting and watching time go by, being late (an hour, a day, a week) is not a grievous offence. This prioritization of affiliation or relationships is an important characteristic of event time societies. In Mexico time walks while in the USA and Britain it either runs or flies.

Edward Hall, an anthropologist who studied the understanding of time, describes event time societies as having polychronic or P-time scheduling.[7] Event time people have a tendency to do several things at once. Various tasks will be on the go at the same time and any given task will be started, suspended and completed along with the others. In P-time, progress occurs a little at a time on several fronts. In western societies, women are supposed to be P-time people, able to juggle various tasks at once, while men work in a linear, sequential manner – monochronic or M-time.

In polychronic societies, a high degree of affiliation and a willingness to give time to relationships is demonstrated at meals. Polychronic societies cook in such a manner that there is usually enough food for the unexpected guest. Food is not critically dependent, as in so much western cooking, on timing and it is less prone to spoil. It is often shared physically by picking off each other's plates or bowls, rather than the carefully apportioned and discrete platefuls typical in British society.

In P-time societies, business people break off their telephone conversations to welcome staff who come into their offices instead of simply gesturing to them with the wave of a hand. People in modern P-time societies have watches and clocks, but they live with a communal sense of time. As Edward Hall explains:

> Polychronic cultures are by their very nature oriented to people. Any human being who is naturally drawn to other human beings and who lives in a world dominated by human relationships will be either pushed or pulled toward the polychronic end of the time spectrum. If you value people, you must hear them out and cannot cut them off simply because of a schedule.
>
> M-time, on the other hand, is oriented to tasks, schedules, and procedures. As anyone who has had experience with bureaucracies knows, schedules and procedures take on a life all their own without reference to either logic or human needs ... M-time is also tangible; we speak of it as

being saved, spent, wasted, lost, made up, crawling, killed, and running out.[8]

The problem for many people is that they are M-time types working in P-time organizations, or vice versa. The tension between P-time and M-time is proving hard to resolve. 'What particularly distinguishes man in contemporary society from his forebears is that he has become increasingly time conscious. The moment we rouse ourselves from sleep we usually wonder what time it is... In previous ages most people worked hard but worried less about time than we do'.[9]

Clock time or M-time

Clock time, or monochronic time, is the time of industrial society, based on the metronomic beating of a universal oscillator. The caesium atom's natural frequency was formally recognized as the new international unit of time in 1967: the second was defined as exactly 9,192,631,770 oscillations or cycles of the caesium atom's resonant frequency. This new definition replaced the previous standard, which was based on the length of time that light took to travel a metre. The move to a time standard based on the oscillations of the caesium atom, which has nothing to do with the motion of the earth, marked the triumph of clock time.

Lewis Mumford described the mechanical clock rather than the steam engine as 'the key machine' of the modern world.[10] The changes it brought were revolutionary:

the clock brought order and control, both collective and personal. Its public display and private possession laid the basis for temporal autonomy: people could now co-ordinate comings and goings without dictation from above. The clock provided punctuation marks for group activity, while enabling individuals to order their own work (and that of others) so as to enhance productivity. The very notion of productivity is the by-product of the clock: once one can relate performance to uniform time units work is never the same. One moves from the task-oriented time consciousness of the peasant (one job after another as time and light permit) and the time-filling busyness of the domestic servant (always something to do) to an effort to maximise product per unit of time (time is money).[11]

Until the Industrial Revolution jobs as such barely existed. People did whatever tasks needed to be done. E.P. Thompson charted the transition from the biblical[12] task orientation of event time to contemporary clock time and described how free English workers were turned into disciplined industrial labourers through an Industrial Revolution that depended on the clock to organize factory work.

The clock makes it possible to co-ordinate people's activities. Without it, the only times that everyone can understand and adhere to are sunrise and sunset, and even then there is scope for considerable variation. But it goes further than that. The mechanical clock introduced a standard time. Employers and workers had a common basis for measuring time and the ability to use it as a medium of exchange.

Instead of being paid for the task, workers during the Industrial Revolution began to be paid for their time. The clock became a measure not only of time but also of money. Workers' time became a commodity to be bought and sold. As E.P. Thompson says, 'Time has become a currency which we spend instead of pass.'[13] Once this happened, there was increasing pressure by the buyers of time, the employers, to maximize the value they obtained from the workers who were the suppliers of time.

Modern attitudes to industrial employees' time are exemplified by the Oxford's clothes factory (in Monticello, Georgia, USA). A system clocks every worker's pace to a thousandth of a minute. The workers, mostly women, are paid according to how their pace compares with a factory standard for their job. Operators who beat the standard by 10 per cent are paid a 10 per cent bonus over their base rate. If they lag 10 per cent behind the standard, they have 10 per cent knocked off their wages.

Quality is now measured by time. Speed has become equated with excellence. It is something we come up against in early life as soon as we begin school. The American economist Jeremy Rifkin's remarks about the USA are just as apposite in general in the UK, where teachers' discretion has been replaced by a standard national curriculum to be absorbed in a set time.

> In our educational system, a premium is placed on how fast we can recite an answer or solve a problem… Keeping up requires quick absorption of material and even faster recall. Children are taught to compete with the clock in classrooms across the country. Exams are cued to time deadlines and achievement is measured by how many answers can be completed in the time allotted. Our society is unwavering in its belief that intelligence and speed go together and that the bright child is always the fastest learner.[14]

The business culture that dominates Britain also equates speed with quality. UK businesses do not tend to reward people for asking questions but rather those who provide quick answers. It is a culture that often descends into the 'quick fix' and the use of the instant cosmetic of public relations rather than the harder and time-consuming work of analysis and consideration.

While it is wrong to set up a dichotomy between clock time and event time given that most societies are neither exclusively one nor the other, the distinctions are instructive. Allowing for the gross simplifications involved, the contrasts are mainly as follows:

- Clock time is individualistic, event time is collective
  Individualistic cultures are geared towards achievement, usually measured by economic success. This 'time is money thinking' is most evident in North America and Britain. In event time cultures, time is given to relationships and there is more concern about family and friends and a generally keener awareness of collective well-being.
- Clock time is linear, event time is cyclical
  A key concept in western thinking is that we start to die from the moment we are born. Time has a direction and the Judaeo-Christian tradition believes that the future will be better than the past. Event time societies tend to think of time as cyclical, constantly returning to earlier stages and starting over again.
- Clock time is abstract, event time is organic
  Time in clock time societies is the product of an electromechanical device. Switch off the device and you have switched off time. In event

time societies, time is intimately connected to natural phenomena and the rituals and work patterns of daily life.
- Clock time is dynamic, event time is static
  Industrial development and clock time are intimately linked while event time is associated with agrarian societies. While there may be value judgements as to which society is preferable, clock time is a society of change while event time societies move at a far slower pace.

The clock fetishism adhered to in Britain is of increasingly doubtful value in a changing society and its rigidity is one of the underlying reasons for the time sickness of today. Clock time is essential for the efficient use of resources and economic growth. But whether it is the most effective means of regulating a late industrial society that is fast becoming a service-dominated economy is another matter. 'As long as we remain part of a society that is structured to the time of clocks and calendars our activities and interactions with others can only escape its pervasive hold to a very limited extent'.[15]

Culture defeats nature

The move from event to clock time has been described as a change in the relationship between Nature and Culture.[16] For much of human history, Nature was dominant. Life was a battle for survival against the natural elements and social systems developed as a means of improving those chances. Our social systems were rooted in our biology. The sun and the moon dictated time and the pattern of daily life.

From the seventeenth century onwards the combination of the free inquiry of thought and experimentation of the Age of Reason and its expression in the inventive genius of the Industrial Revolution led to a new social age, one where social relations were largely rooted in the world of work. The clock came into its own as the regulator of the industrial age. In this period Culture began to dominate Nature. Time and space collapsed as distance disappeared; this happened slowly at first with the invention of the steam train and then more quickly with the advent of the telegraph, telephone, the car, the jet plane and now with the instantaneous transmission available with fax, email, pager and videophone. In the year 2000, a quarter of the world's telephone subscribers will have mobile phones, enabling them to be in touch 24 hours a day if they wish.[17] BT will introduce a new phone before the year 2000 that will act as a cordless phone within the home and a cellular phone within 300 metres or more from its base. Early in the twenty-first century, nearly all new phones will have this dual capability so vastly increasing the numbers of mobile phone subscribers.

We are now in a completely new age. Yet we have difficulty in accepting this change. We still behave as though there is a natural world that begins when the sun rises and closes as it sets, and our days are still structured in this way. The workplace still dominates our lives and determines our social relations. If you ask people what they do, the answer is invariably in the form of a job function, not a lifestyle choice. Yet we are going to have to adapt to a new world in which our social relations are shaped not by nature, nor by the work we do but by cultural choices. Until now, our shared experiences are based on place – where we grew up, who we went to school with, where we worked and so on. These experiences were based on physical connections. Now, we inhabit a cyberspace where

> time, history and memory become qualitatively different concepts. Instead of relating to the past through a shared sense of place or ancestry, consumers of electronic mass media can experience a common heritage with people they have never seen; they can acquire memories of a past to which they have no geographical or biological connection. This capacity of electronic communication to transcend time and space creates instability by disconnecting people from past traditions, but it also liberates people by making the past less determinate of experiences in the present.[18]

Controlling time

Nearly all of us have experienced those elusive moments when time stands still and we feel in control. We can become so absorbed in what we are doing and concentrating on the immediate task that time no longer matters. Bungee jumpers who say that time seems to freeze and stand still are onto something. Time plays tricks. Tennis players often refer to entering the 'zone', a state in which they feel they have all the time in the world to hit a ball. Artists frequently describe the hours as flying by when they work, so engrossed are they in the immediate task. This happy state has been labelled 'flow' by Mihaly Csikszentmihalyi, an American psychology professor who has turned flow into the new management buzz-word.

Since the mid-1960s, Csikszentmihalyi has been studying states of what he calls 'optimal experience' – the times when people report feelings of concentration and deep enjoyment. The metaphor of 'flow' is one that many people have used to describe the sense of effortless action they feel in moments that stand out as the best in their lives. It seems to happen most when people are subjected neither to extreme time pressure nor extreme boredom. We are happiest in the time sense when we are doing things that are moderately challenging and that engage our skills.

Some Americans, as expected, take the whole notion of flow a bit too far. Orion Moshe Kopelman is a Silicon Valley industrialist who has published a book called *The Second Ten Commandments*. Number one in the new list is 'Maximize your time spent in flow and happiness', which does not have quite the same ring as 'I am the Lord Thy God, thou shalt have no other Gods before me'.[19]

THE ENTREPRENEUR

Calvin Pike never slept much even as a kid. 'I used to sing to myself when I went to bed, and often I would still be singing at 2 a.m. I just never needed that much sleep. In fact, I have always felt a little frustrated that I have to sleep at all.'

Now he manages on about five hours a night which is useful because the other nineteen hours are soon accounted for. He is managing director of PKR, a start-up company that began in 1994 the business of educational training, inspection, consultancy and personnel. In the first year, his company carried out two school inspections. They performed six in the second year, twenty in the third and two hundred and sixty in the fourth. From two part-time staff at the start, in 1998 there were twenty-two full-time employees and dozens of certified freelance school inspectors, education trainers and consultants. Running the business keeps him busy for twelve hours a day, six days a week.

Then there is time to be spent with his wife and two young boys. And he is working through to a doctorate in educational management.

For him five hours sleep a night seems excessive, so about once a week Pike works through the night. He describes it as 'a session when I try to put things together'.

> I make lists and do all that sort of time-management activity, but what works best for me is that around 2 a.m. all the thoughts in my head seem to crystalize and I can start getting a handle on things. Often, I lose all track of time and it is only when my wife brings me a cup of tea at around 7 a.m. that I realize I have been up all night.

This self-induced flow state may have something to do with his having once taken a course in self-hypnosis. The idea was to induce a relaxed state in which problems and issues would be resolved. It seems to work in his case. It may also be that Pike is something of an owl, preferring to work during the evening and night. As a young language teacher he worked in Italy. 'The hours were 10 to 12 in the morning and then a long break before working from 5 until 9 in the evening. That really suited me.'

Flow has been associated with time-free thinking typical of the right hemisphere of the brain. The brain's cerebrum is divided in two halves, a left and a right hemisphere connected by the 200 million nerve fibres and is known as the corpus callosum. No other mammal except the human being is known to have a so-called hemisphere specialization, two seemingly symmetrical halves with different approaches to the same subject, a digital and an analogic. In most cases the two hemispheres are characterized by the left being the digital (rational, verbal and analytic perception and thinking) and the right the analogic ('seeing the larger perspective', sensoric, creative).

This fits with the idea of the clock as the first example of a digital device.[20] The clock counted a regular, repeating sequence such as a pendulum swing rather than tracking a continuous, regular motion such as a shadow moving on a sundial or the flow of water. These were analogue devices.

The clock is representative of a digital society which is based on the binary system that underlies western thinking. In the binary code of 0s and 1s, everything is either on or off. There are no in-betweens, no 'fuzzy' states of being. This goes back to Aristotle and his introduction of classification which places everything into neat categories. Pigeon-hole thinking is a powerful tool for organizing the world so that it is comprehensible. But it introduces hard edges into a natural world that is soft-edged and messy. Bart Kosko, who has written the definitive introduction to fuzzy logic, pointed out that Aristotle founded the system of teaching in which we grow up today.[21] What is the answer to the question? Hands up or hands down. The answer is right or wrong. We do not handle partial answers, an arm neither up nor down. We divide the world up into arbitrary groups; say those under 30 and those over, married and unmarried, time pressured and not time pressured, night and day, morning and evening.

The world is not binary. It is messy and fuzzy. Try answering the question: are you married? There is a strictly legal definition that depends on having a certificate but the human answers might vary from 'very much so' to 'sort of' to 'I suppose so' with thousands of other variants. Capturing the sheer complexity of human life and the blurring of all the edges requires a different way of thinking than the binary approach we are used to.

Kosko explains the idea behind fuzzy thinking by describing eating an apple:

> Hold an apple in your hand. Is it an apple? Yes. The object in your hand belongs to the clumps of space-time we call the set of apples – all apples anywhere ever. Now take a bite, chew it, swallow it. Let your digestive tract take apart the apple's molecules. Is the object in your hand still an apple? Yes or no? Take another bite. Is the new object in your hand still an apple? Take another bite, and so on down to void.
>
> The apple changes from thing to non-thing, to nothing. But where does it cross the line from apple to non-apple? When you hold half an apple in your hand, the apple is as much there as not. The half apple foils all-or-none descriptions. The half apple is a fuzzy apple, the grey between the black and the white. Fuzziness is greyness.'[22]

Grasp that and you have the basic understanding behind fuzzy logic. You also hold the profound difference between the thinking of Aristotle and the Buddha. Aristotle said, 'Everything must be or not be, whether in the present or in the future'.[23] Living in India five centuries before Christ, the Buddha taught, 'I have not explained that the world is eternal or not eternal. I have not explained that the world is finite or infinite.'[24] It is a philosophy of connectedness and concentrates on ambivalence as opposed to the bivalence at the heart of western thinking.

Juxtaposing event time and clock time is useful for analysis, but it falls into the Aristotelian trap of either–or rather than considering the question of degree. If we can spring that trap then we can begin to think beyond the confines of currently imposed time and its constructs into a different frame that meets needs at the end of the century.

At a social level the best mix is not one of time pressure or time surfeit but a combination of the two. Parents with complex, challenging and stimulating jobs are more likely to be warm and responsive at home than their peers in less demanding or unfulfilling work.[25] It is not so much the case of incessant demands upon one's time that is the problem, but the state of mind in which those demands are handled.

> You need to see it as 24 hour life not 24 hour strife. If there are no limits to the beginning and the end of the day, then we no longer have to squeeze things in. We create more space, which means we don't feel guilty about taking time to exercise, or have a chat with friends. As soon as you set limits on things you set up a negative dynamic, setting yourself up for wilful abuse of the limits and guilt.[26]

A company that epitomizes the new way of thinking is First Direct, the telephone bank. First Direct explains itself by noting that when it opened in 1989 it broke two barriers, one of space and one of time. The bank has no retail branches and is available for use 24 hours a day, 365 days a year. In an inadvertent but classic piece of fuzzy logic, the bank's literature says 'First Direct is not important because it is open at 2.00 a.m, but because it is not closed at 2.00 a.m.'

In the world of fuzzy logic, open and closed are not the binary opposites of classical thinking. Open and closed are two ends of a spectrum containing many intermediate states. That is what the 24 hour world is about. It is not about rigid times denoted by the clock but rather it is a fluid and dynamic conception of time incorporating an infinite range of possibilities.

6 Flexible time

*People work round the clock these days, especially in Soho with all the media
companies, so we need to cater for that. If people finish work at midnight and want to
have breakfast and a drink we should be able to provide for that.*

David Talans, Soho bar owner[1]

In the nineteenth century, the shift from an agricultural to an industrial
society resulted in the transformation of a society that lived its life by
event time, run by the timing of the natural world into one of clock time,
dominated by the mechanical clock. This has dislocated our relationship
with time and new time patterns have to emerge. The 24 Hour Society is a
flexible response to the reshaping of the world, in its own way as dramatic a
change as the move from event time to clock time. It provides us with a
better way to manage our time.

Managing time is one of the conditions of the age. There is no family calendar stuck on the fridge door with magnets in the home of Eric Benhamour,
chief executive of 3Com, a Silicon Valley company. Instead, he and his family
go through a daily cyber-ritual of uploading the day's schedules from their
palm-top computers.[2] This hi-tech solution may not, in truth, solve any of
their scheduling problems, but it probably makes the Benhamour family feel
that they are managing time efficiently.

Likewise, the young obsessives who work on the world's money exchanges
have video screens displaying constantly updated equity and futures prices
built into the machines which they work out on at the gym. It may make
little or no difference to their trading, but it gives the impression that not a
second is being wasted.

The seriously rich have never had a problem managing their time. With
cooks, butlers, chauffeurs and maids to do the chores there are far more
hours available in the day. It is said that the Queen has never run a bath in

her life. It is the 99.9 per cent of the population who are not seriously rich who struggle daily, coping with the lack of time left in the day after work, cleaning, dropping the children off at school, preparing meals and all the other mundane tasks that make up living.

Siamack Salari makes his living documenting the struggle of ordinary people juggling their tasks to fit into the available hours. A young Iranian with a background in design and ergonomics, he is the proverbial fly on the wall. As head of London advertising agency BMP's Culture Lab, his job is to observe people at home, work, shopping and play. He and his team live with volunteer families, watching and analysing their behaviour. Most of the work is for commercial organizations, concerned with how and why people buy goods and services. 'We stipulate that we have to sleep there for the duration of the project. The idea is to get a complete picture of how people live and to match what they do with what they say.' As a result he has a great deal of material relating to time use.

Salari confirms what is known from other sources. Even if both adults are working, it is the woman who does most of the housework. But what his studies also show is how much negotiation goes on about time in families.

> Adding a time dimension often occurs when the woman is talking. So she will say, 'Can you do that for me, it will only take five minutes.' It seldom works the other way round. In many ways, most of the conversation between the adults in the family, which is usually initiated by the woman, revolves around managing time. It is a crucial element in their lives.

Supermarket shopping particularly interests Salari and his team.

> You may have noticed that clocks in supermarkets are not very prominent, if there at all. This is all part of a general attempt to remove all external cues and create a controlled environment. We found that supermarket shoppers are about 30–40 per cent out when asked to assess how long they had been in the shop, so someone saying they had been in the shop for half an hour had in fact been there for forty-five minutes or longer.

A key finding is how working mothers in particular try to plan out their day, based around inflexible events such as school delivery and collection. If something gets out of kilter in the schedule, say a hold up in traffic or a lengthy wait in a doctor's surgery, there is a domino effect that brings down the whole of the day's time structure. 'It can be so bad', Salari says, 'that the rest of the day is effectively written off. The time rituals that women construct to get them through their juggling routine are extremely sensitive.'

On the other side of London, in Smithfield, Michael Willmott of the Future Foundation is busy classifying how people relate to time. Using a mathematical technique known as 'fuzzy clustering' to analyse market research data, he has come up with four types of time users:

1. **Fast laners (25 per cent of adults)**: these are the people who enjoy the 24 hour culture. They tend to be under 30 and without children. They feel fairly time pressured but do not think that the pace of life is too fast and they believe that their lives would be enhanced if services were available 24 hours a day. Their view of the 24 Hour Society is hedonistic and bound up with the immediate satisfaction of their wants.

2. **Convenience driven (28 per cent of adults)**: this is the family group, the 30–50 year olds, often of two working parents with dependent children. This group is the most time pressured (over 90 per cent), who also complain that the pace of life is too fast. They are very much in favour of 24 hour service which they see as a pragmatic solution to some of their time problems.

3. **Pressured conservatives (19 per cent of adults)**: this is a middle-aged group with older children. They feel some time pressures and that the pace of life is too fast (but both at lower levels than the convenience driven). They do not support 24 hour service and think of it as unnecessary, taking a somewhat moralistic line about its desirability.

4. **Past timers (27 per cent of adults)**: this is an older age group, most of whom are 60 years old or above and whose children have left home. The large majority are retired and as a group they do not themselves feel time pressured but believe the world is now moving too fast. They see no need for 24 hour service; rather, they would like the world to slow down and be like it was in the past.

Willmott believes that the trend towards the 24 Hour Society will continue and intensify as it is driven by three consumer factors: the younger age groups who now support it will probably retain that feeling as they age; working parents are going to be time pressured whatever else happens; and the idea of immediacy which has taken root now that people expect and demand immediate response.

The key people pushing the demand for a 24 Hour Society are the 30–50 year olds' convenience-driven group. Even though they often feel that life is moving too fast, they are looking for solutions to their time problems, rather than attempting to change their lifestyles by down-shifting. They are prepared to pay a price premium for the convenience provided by 24 hour opening which gives them flexibility in managing their time. They also accept that their time problems can be helped by better time management. The 24 Hour Society makes it easier for them to organize their time, but they still require the individual skills and disciplines of time management.

One of the difficulties of time management stems from the non-fungibility of time. Fungibility is an idea used in economics which effectively states that money, for example, has no labels. A pound is a pound, wherever it comes from. But people do not behave like that. Some money is more sacrosanct than others. So people with money on deposit will leave it where it is and borrow on their credit cards at high interest rates. The money on deposit is felt to be inviolate and cannot be touched, it is somehow different from credit card borrowings. In technical terms, the marginal propensity to consume all types of wealth is not equal.

If a pound is not exactly like every other pound in the consumer mind, so a minute is not like every other minute. The notion of quality time is intuitively understood and suggests a difference in intensity from normal time. Likewise, at times people feel they can relax, at others they fret and feel that they should be doing something more productive with their time. Our time is context dependent. Sometimes, it can be wasted; at other times it cannot.

Each of us has what might be termed a mental time account. This makes it hard to act as rationally as time management suggests. We behave according to mood, which is linked to our biological rhythms, often to our own detriment. It is possible to reschedule someone's time so that they are more efficient, but it is far more difficult to tailor their time use to their mental states and make them more effective.

THE TIME MANAGER

Jayne Stoddart is a typical example of the time-pressured, convenience-driven adult. She has a 4-year-old daughter and a 6-month-old baby, she was a former county netball player and still plays competitively, and she is a senior executive responsible for a turnover of £2.6 million and a staff of twenty in peak periods. She is the head of the division that markets the time planners and other paper-based products of TMI International, Britain's leading time-management company. If she cannot handle it then nobody can.

> When I went back to work after my first child, I was determined to show that I could combine being a mother with a career. I was very tough-minded. After the second child I did not feel that I had to prove it in the same way. I was much more relaxed. I have learned that you cannot be perfect. It is not possible to be the perfect mother, the perfect wife, the perfect manager. That is the main value of time management; it teaches you to set realistic objectives for what you need to do and what you want to do. But I could not have done any of it without my mother-in-law, who looks after both children now and my husband. And it is easier for me as an executive than it is for my team, who have much more rigid work schedules. But then, they do not have to stay on for meetings and I can never say 'I have done my forty hours so I am off now.'

Each weekday morning she drops the children off at about 8 a.m. and then picks them up after work around 6 p.m. Having secure and reliable child-care is the main thing. She has enough flexibility in her working day to get the odd things she needs, though having a chemist who closes for lunch is something of a nuisance. Her husband does the weekly shop, usually on a Saturday evening or Sunday morning.

She and her husband share the housework, though she observes there is a difference in the way they operate.

> If I cook, I will clear up as I go along. When he does, he actually makes a better job of it, but he leaves all the clearing up until the end. I think men get more focused on what they are doing but they cannot handle the juggling that women have to cope with. When you have children you are continually at their beck and call and doing many tasks at once. Men are not as good at doing that. Women are forever picking things up and putting things away; men seem to be able to live with it.

Jayne's netball training is on Tuesday nights and she plays every other Saturday. It needs organization, considering that she and her husband are also renovating their Solihull home. What she needs is not so much late-opening shops but rather some time in the day when she can sit quietly and do the necessary domestic and private arranging and thinking. 'Once the children are in bed and asleep it is probably about 9 p.m. and you are too tired to start sorting bills and all that. It would be helpful to have a place at work where you could spend half an hour in the lunch break doing all that. With no telephones ringing.'

Individual time management is useful but it is not a structural solution to a structural problem. Most organizations operate under the M-time pattern discussed in Chapter 5. M-time and P-time do not coexist well.[3] M-time individuals are naturally happier and more productive in M-time organizations while P-time people do better in P-time ones. Yet it is doubtful how closely organisations in Britain look at their time cultures and question their effectiveness. Individual time management is about individual efficiency, but if we are going to beat the time problem, then the flexibility offered by the 24 Hour Society has to apply not just to individuals but to organizations as well.

Flexible hours and flexible firms

One way of reducing the job-stress inherent in a globally competitive system is the introduction of more flexible work practices. In the UK 43 per cent of a sample of adult full and part-time workers said they would welcome the opportunity to choose how to organize a set number of hours of work: only 20 per cent said they were able to do so.[4] A survey by *Management Today* found that working flexible hours was third on the list of desirable changes, following working fewer hours in the first place and changing the company culture.[5] The fact that 63 per cent felt that putting in long hours was confused with commitment suggests that companies may well be leaner and meaner but not necessarily working smarter. However, the same survey showed that despite their unhappiness with the time balance in their lives, less than a quarter would be prepared to accept lower pay for more time in their personal life.

Some British companies are starting to recognize these time pressures and have begun offering time-saving services to their employees. Rolls Royce Bristol runs a shop, offering among other things dry-cleaning services. Dupont in Gloucester is one of many companies that has a cashpoint machine to save employees having to go to the bank. Employees at the British Airways Waterside complex can buy flowers and gifts at the shops on the main street.

Other ways of finding and managing time include introducing far more flexibility to working hours. Employees in a Dutch nursing home draw up their own work rotas by agreement among themselves. In a British aircraft manufacturing company, nine workers are responsible for maintaining the machinery on a 24 hour basis, Monday to Friday. The workers can fix times to suit themselves and can rearrange their shifts. At the Dupont Gloucestershire plant, the nylon fibre manufacturer agreed with workers that they could arrange their working hours so long as the required number of staff were on duty at any one time.

Among full-time core employees, the movement is towards annualized hours contracts, ensuring that staff are working flexibly to meet the peaks and troughs of demand. Instead of working a fixed number of hours a week, employees on an annualized hours contract work a fixed number of hours a year.

Redditch Council in Worcestershire has an annualized hours contract with its gardening staff. There is obviously more work to do in summer than winter, but the way the workforce was organized meant that in summer the council had to bring in extra outside contractors during peak times. A new annualized hours system was introduced in the winter of 1994. The men work four days a week in winter, half having Monday off and the other half taking Friday off. In summer, the working week is correspondingly longer. The system has virtually removed the need for contractors and after the initial teething period has proved popular with the workforce.

BMW has considerable experience operating sophisticated flexible working patterns in its German factories including an annualized hours system that it calls a working time account. The company operates some 300 flexibility packages covering different plants and groups of workers. To maximize machine use, BMW believes 'human labour hours and machine operating times must be separated from one another. The only way to reach this objective is by introducing flexible, plant-related working time models and regulations'.[6]

Since 1989, workers at BMW's Regensburg plant have worked nine-hour shifts on a two-shift pattern, which means an effective four-day week for each worker within the plant's six-day week. This is claimed to increase productivity by 25 per cent over a conventional two-shift pattern. At the Munich plant, the workers do an extra thirty-five minutes a day but get a long weekend every five weeks. BMW says that plant operating hours are up 8 per cent without extra capital investment.

BMW is expecting to introduce similar flexible working arrangements at its Rover plants in the UK. The German company also makes extensive use of part-time workers. About 2,500 employees in Germany work less than the general working week. The number of part-time workers has risen 40 per cent since 1996; half the part-time workers are men.

Since the late 1970s, the proportion of part-time workers in Britain has doubled to around 6.5 million. One in four employees works part-time. This is likely to rise to one in three in the year 2000. Part-time work has tended in the past to be low skilled, poorly paid and often insecure. Eight in ten part-timers are women, many of them mothers who find child-care too expensive for full-time work. Many have been exploited because of this. Some employers at least recognize that there are people who wish to limit their hours of work and that their needs can be accommodated into the overall work pattern. Dennis Foster works part-time for 25.5 hours a week on a rolling shift system with morning, afternoon and evening shifts each week. He is one of a team employed by Norwich Council to operate a 24 hour, 365 day a year telephone alarm cover for 7,000 elderly people who live alone. Part-time work suits his lifestyle as he is also an artist and sculptor.

The growth in higher education and less generous state financing has contributed to the rise in part-time working. A quarter of all students now work part-time and in Britain we are moving fast to the American practice of using students as an important, floating part of the labour force. Sainsburys employs 26,000 students, a quarter of its workforce, to cover trading peaks on Thursday and Friday evenings and over the weekend.

In 1990, there were three quarters of a million students in England and Wales. By 1996, the numbers had grown by 50 per cent, to over 1.2 million. The large increase in the number of students is an important driver of the 24 Hour Society. Students spend a greater proportion of their income in cafés and pubs than the rest of the adult population. Leicester, which has 25,000 students out of a total population of 300,000 students is typical of many towns where students are now an important part of the local economy as both consumers and producers. Belvoir Street in Leicester is the town's new café quarter. Its existence owes as much to changing patterns in education and employment as it does to changing tastes. Students provide the bulk of the cheap and flexible workforce required by bars and restaurants.

A growing but unclassified proportion of people who wish to limit their hours may be those who are looking after an elderly parent. Some, known as the sandwich generation as they are caught in the middle, have responsibilities for both children and parents. A few employers are beginning to recognize the time pressure put on staff with caring responsibilities. In a pioneering move in conjunction with motor industry charities, Peugeot has established a special centre for the elderly parents of workers at the Coventry plant. The centre caters for varying levels of physical and mental disability and enables employees to bring their parent to the centre, allowing them to continue working while still undertaking heavy caring responsibilities.

But few employers have followed Peugeot's initiative and are prepared to help their workforce balance their work and home lives. Although a 1996 Department of Education and Employment survey found that 65 per cent of employers claim to offer some kind of family-friendly working arrangements, including part-time working, only 10 per cent provided any practical help with child-care.

A Danish study found that in a workplace based on co-operation between employees and emphasis on groups and teams, the general environment and approach to flexibility was positive. Employees were able to organize their work-time in sympathy with their domestic lives. Where the career structure favoured direct or indirect competition between employees, the environment was hostile towards flexibility even if the company made the appropriate noises. [7]

If flexibility is not grounded into an organization and is not part of its basic systems, then it will be a contingent add-on, ditched at the first difficulty in the same way as health promotion and 'healthy' activities. In that case, 24 hour working will not be a liberating act, enabling employees to structure their work and domestic lives with more freedom. Instead, the organization will attempt to extract longer working hours from the workforce and pay little attention to the effects of shift-working. In this context, the EU Working Hours Directive, now part of British law, may play a key role in developing a beneficial 24 Hour Society by extending operating hours without extending individual working hours.

In effect, there is a double whammy that is driving the world towards a 24 Hour Society. In a shrinking manufacturing sector competing on a global basis, there is intense pressure to get the maximum return from the fixed costs tied up in the business. This points towards continual 24 hour factory working. At the same time, the burgeoning services sector in a deregulated environment has to be open when the demand is there. This is one of the lessons to be drawn from Sunday opening.

The emphasis on speed and time is driven both by customer demands and the need to cut costs. Reducing waste and inefficiency is virtually guaranteed to speed things up. Just-in-time manufacturing cuts inventory stocks in the factory from days to hours by integrating supplier systems with those of the final assembly plant. It is being extended to the factory output in what is known as just-in-time distribution. Just-in-time talent is the means by which people are employed on an as-necessary basis, supplied by companies such as Manpower. Instead of employing their own staff, companies increasingly outsource requirements to contract providers.

In the workplace, the key is to manage time pressure without succumbing to time stress. The former is challenging, requiring self-organization, and is helped by flexible and extended hours in a 24 hour world. It needs a robust frame of mind and the feeling of being able to maintain control.

Time stress is pathological and creates physical and mental health problems resulting in poor sleep, panic attacks, and feelings of general malaise. Whatever the causal reasons, once time pressure tips over into time stress then 24 hour opening and time management are of little help. Management of this condition probably requires external help in the form of counselling and stress-reduction activities. In the longer term what may be needed is a different form of work environment. Flexible working offers a whole range of opportunities but if they employ people to work during off-peak hours, organizations will have to balance internal efficiency with genuine concern for employees.

7 The rhythm of life

I not long ago asked a friend, an Englishman, if he naps. 'Whenever possible,' he replied. Prone or sitting up? 'Prone.' On a bed or couch? 'Bed.' Trousers on or off? 'Generally off.' And for how long? 'That depends,' he said, 'on when the cats choose to depart.'

'Aristides', *The American Scholar*[1]

Enlightened Technologies is an American company with an unusual product. It claims to sell sleep. This is not some fly-by-night outfit offering a potion collected from a rare crocodile found only in the upper reaches of the Orinoco but a genuine hi-tech start-up headed by reputable scientists commercializing the new and hot scientific specialism known as chronobiology.

Enlightened Technologies is working on a simple and portable light-based appliance that can resynchronize the biological rhythms that programme us to sleep at night and be awake in daytime. The device, when fully developed, will probably look like a normal pair of spectacles but with a thicker rim. A small power pack that can be carried in a pocket or clipped to a belt transmits light via an opto-electronic cable to fibre optics embedded in the lenses. The pattern of light delivered to selected parts of the eye changes as the eye moves. The lenses will be made up to the user's normal prescription so all the person has to do is wear the spectacles for an hour or so in the evening while reading or watching television and the programmed delivery of light will reset the circadian rhythms.

These daily or circadian rhythms control a variety of physiological processes, including body temperature, blood pressure, hormone production, urination, digestion and sleep itself. By harmonizing these processes, circadian rhythms control the way our bodies and minds function. At night most of us are far worse at performing tasks that involve manual dexterity or mental arithmetic for example. Our reaction times are slower and our ability to reason and make decisions is considerably reduced. Battles started just before sunrise to catch the enemy literally napping.

The basic circadian rhythm that separates night from day has been fundamental to us ever since the times of our primitive hunter-gatherer ancestors. We now live in a controlled environment and spend most of our waking hours in an artificial light that is considerably less bright than sunlight. This presents a particular problem among older people. It is estimated that one-third of people over 50 have disturbed or inadequate sleep as result of their sleep–wake rhythm getting out of kilter. Resetting the rhythms with very bright light brings them back into line. At least that is the theory.

There are over one hundred circadian rhythms that have a period of about 24 hours. Other cycles have time periods ranging from fractions of a second to years. The menstrual cycle is the best known of the twenty-eight-day hormone cycles that affect both men and women. The 120,000 or so hair follicles on the human scalp also grow in cycles. Each follicle enters a growing cycle that may last from eighteen months to three to five years. The follicle then rests for three months before starting the growth cycle again. The cycles are staggered so that about 10 per cent of follicles are resting at any one time. An astonishing annual cycle was that of a male red deer on the Isle of Rhum. Named Aristotle by visiting scientists, he shed his antlers on the same day plus or minus one every year for ten years.[2] Other cycles recur every seven years – as Joseph demonstrated to the Pharaoh. Some of these cycles are a response to environmental changes such as changes in temperature, others are regulated by an internal timer.

An organism's physiological processes interact in a wild cacophony of cycles and feedbacks that are managed by a complex mix of central and local controls. Integral to this control is the notion of the internal timer, the ticking clock whose beat is the rhythm of life on this planet. Biological rhythms and biological clocks are found in all plants and animals and are fundamental components of biological organisms. The ubiquity of such rhythms suggests that they are both ancient and essential. They are organisms' response to environmental cues that come and go with the earth's movements, such as the rising and setting of the sun. The sleep researcher Professor Walter J. Schwartz describes 'all biological clocks as adaptations to life on a rotating world.'[3] According to Schwartz, biological clocks have two functions. They permit awareness of local change, acting like a sundial that records the time in a specific place, and they also measure the passage of time, like an hourglass: 'This allows the organism to maintain an internal temporal order and to anticipate change. If you are a mouse, it is useful to be able to anticipate when an eagle will fly and already be in your burrow, rather than be caught scurrying into it.' It makes sense and there is survival value in being able to predict sunrise and generally know when the immediate environment is going to change.

But as one of the pioneers in circadian research has pointed out, while there has been much research as to the purpose of these rhythms, it is 'a substantial mystery' as to why biological clocks evolved.[4] We can speculate about the possible advantages but there are no absolutely clear-cut reasons. But then evolution does not proceed by reasoned steps. Living things are not designed. They are the products of chance and small reproductive advantage that results from an improved fit with the immediate environment.

For example, having two ears is useful but a well-designed person would have at least three and probably more. Then we would be able to hear sounds in different planes and be able to 'focus' our hearing at will. Likewise, we would be much better off if we had several eyes.

> Evolution never designs anything from scratch. It can only tinker with whatever happens to be already there. Much of anatomical human nature derives not from anything currently desirable but from adaptive changes made in the early history of vertebrates. Many of the most obvious such features date back to the initial establishment of bilateral symmetry. Many anatomical structures are either single midline organs, or they come in pairs, one member to the left, another to the right.[5]

Thus we have two arms and two legs not for any good functional reason, but because the early fishes that dragged themselves out onto land were bilaterally symmetrical and had two fins on each side that eventually became limbs. Six limbs would have been better, as anyone who uses a word processor with a mouse and tries to drink a cup of coffee at the same time knows.

We carry a great deal of evolutionary baggage, including sleeping patterns and circadian rhythms, that we are beginning to address only now. The promise of genetic engineering is not only that it corrects the faults inherent in our past but also that it can begin to design a future. We are adjusting to the idea of gene-therapy as a means of negating the effects of deleterious genes such as those involved in cystic fibrosis. There is a slow dawning of realization that we can go further than simply restoring individuals to a healthier condition. We can improve the basic design so that the human model is better adapted. And that includes not only our biological shape but also our physiology, including the biological rhythms and sleep patterns. Provided that great caution is exercised in ensuring that the eugenics shadow does not fall on the potential medical and biological good that can be done, there is the hope of improving the lot of people everywhere. But that is for a still distant, though approaching, future.

Whatever their evolutionary lineage, circadian rhythms affect many areas of activity. In order to understand the natural rhythms of our bodies, it is useful to list some of the main patterns they dictate.

Sleep and wake

It may seem that a person sleeps when tired and wakes when rested. But sleep patterns follow a circadian rhythm. Humans are most likely to sleep soundly when their body temperature is lowest, in the small hours of the morning. Waking is most likely to occur when the temperature starts to rise around 6 to 8 a.m. Experimental animal research and investigation of patients with small tumours has shown that without the internal biological clock, we might sleep twelve hours a day but the timing of the sleep would be random.

As people age, the brain's inner clock loses cells. This changes the circadian rhythms and is especially noticeable in sleep patterns. An older person is likely to nap more, have disrupted sleep and awaken earlier.

Temperature

Body temperature is at its lowest when the body is inactive. Activity can make its temperature rise. But despite these factors, temperature also follows a definite circadian rhythm. In the late afternoon, body temperature can be as much as 1 or more degrees Centigrade higher than in the morning. It will rise and fall even if the person never sees daylight.

Hormone production

Almost all hormones are regulated, to some extent, by circadian rhythms. Cortisol affects many body functions, including metabolism and regulation of the immune system. Its levels are highest between 6 and 8 a.m. and gradually decline throughout the day. Growth hormones stimulate growth in children and help maintain muscle and connective tissue in adults. Sleep triggers the production of these hormones, regardless of the time the onset of sleep occurs. Production peaks during the first two hours of sleep. If a person is deprived of sleep, production drops.

Cardiovascular system

More strokes and heart attacks occur in the morning than at any other time of day. The first hour or two after waking are the most dangerous. These are the peak hours for myocardial infarctions, haemorrhagic strokes, thrombotic infarctions and myocardial ischaemia. This makes some people wonder if morning exercise is safe. However, morning changes in the body – not exercise – may be responsible for cardiovascular problems. Blood clots most rapidly at about 8 a.m. Yet many patients wait an hour or two after they get up to take their medicine. Blood pressure also rises in the morning and stays elevated until late afternoon. Then it drops off and hits its lowest point during the night. But many hypertensive drugs work only for about eighteen to twenty hours.

The changes in the cardiovascular system occur independently of physical activity. Exercise at any time of the day is beneficial. But athletes training for competition may have reason to hope that their event is scheduled later in the day. Athletes seem to perform best in the late afternoon, when strength, body temperature and flexibility peak.

Pain tolerance

Athletes who compete late in the day may also perform better because they can 'gain' without as much 'pain'. Pain tolerance is highest in the afternoon. One study shows that tooth pain is lowest in the late afternoon, which is useful to know when arranging dental appointments.

Medication

Scientists are looking at how circadian rhythms affect the way the body uses medications. Taking medication 'by the clock', known as chronotherapy, helps the drugs work better and reduces their side-effects. Some doctors prescribe night-time administration of medication for patients with ulcer disease or asthma (which worsen at night), rheumatoid arthritis (which worsens in the early morning hours) and high cholesterol levels (most of the body's cholesterol production occurs at night). For patients with osteoarthritis, which worsens in the afternoon and evening, some doctors prescribe midday medication.[6] One finding is that less anaesthesia is needed to cause analgesia or drowsiness when administered in the afternoon.[7] Some cancer treatments are best delivered at carefully selected times in sympathy with the body's circadian cycle so as to minimize side-effects. A Canadian study followed 118 children with acute lymphoblastic leukaemia for eleven years. Once the children were in remission, their parents gave them a daily maintenance dose of chemotherapy at home, either in the morning or evening according to their convenience, but at the same time each day. The researchers found that children receiving their medication in the late afternoon or evening had a threefold greater likelihood of being cured.[8] The timing of chemotherapy in other cancers such as breast cancer also seems to be of critical importance.

The incidence of asthma is rising rapidly. Known as a night-time disease, even with treatment three out of four people with asthma have attacks at least one night a week, and four out of ten have attacks every night. In untreated patients, asthma attacks may occur a hundred times more often at night than during the day. Attacks are most frequent when airways are most constricted, about 4 a.m. in people who sleep at night. When sleep shifts, asthma attacks also shift.

If drugs used in treating asthma, such as theophylline, are taken once a day around 6 to 7 p.m. with supper, this provides a peak level at 3 to 5 a.m. when it is needed, and a lower level in the daytime, when it is not, giving better control than equally divided doses.

However, most primary care providers do not know much about timed dosing, according to the results of a 1996 Gallup physician survey in the USA, which probably would be echoed in Britain. Barely half of the physicians (49 per cent) reported having some familiarity with the concept of chronobiology. Only one in twenty said they were very familiar with chrono-biology. One in four said they did not think chronobiology was important in diagnosis or in the treatment of disease.

Mood

Psychologist David Dinges of the University of Pennsylvania believes that 'some hours of the day we're happier than others and it is occurring inside us, not just in reaction to the world around us.'[9] It seems that our moods are dependent on the circadian rhythms and feeling high or low may be more to do with our internal clocks than anything else. Manipulations of sleep and light exposure may reduce the rapid mood swings and depression that characterize premenstrual dysphoric disorder (PMDD), a severe form of premenstrual syndrome. An estimated 5 per cent of women experience this disorder, with symptoms severe enough to interfere with their ability to function at home or work.

Depriving patients of sleep and shifting sleep to an earlier or later time are all being tried to relieve PMDD, other types of depression, and the emotional swings of menopause. Barbara Parry, a psychiatrist at the University of California, believes that light should also be seen as a drug given that it is physiologically active, and light exposure at specific times of day can be therapeutic for some types of depression. She warns, however, that the research is still preliminary and findings are not yet ready for widespread clinical application.

The 24 Hour Society challenges these natural circadian rhythms. Disrupting our circadian rhythms can have serious effects on our basic physiology:

> our bodies were designed to hunt by day, sleep at night and never travel more than a few dozen miles from sunrise to sunset. Now we work and play at all hours, whisk off by jet to the far side of the world, make life-or-death decisions, or place orders on foreign stock exchanges in the wee small hours of the morning.[10]

However, human beings were never designed in any actual sense and certainly our current bodies are not well adapted to be sedentary for much of the day, eat processed foods, live in centrally heated homes and barely exercise. But we do and we live far longer than those primitive ancestors who had a life expectancy of less than 30 years. Even the hard-exercising, manual-labouring great-grandparents of today's generation were lucky to make it past 45. The past century may have been the bloodiest in human history, but in terms of science and technology, understanding of the human body has progressed enormously.

The drive to discover the workings of the biological clock are rooted in both scientific curiosity and the profound medical and physiological implications that would come from such an understanding of the interplay between biological rhythms and health and sickness. Many of the depressive illnesses, such as manic depression itself, follow a daily rhythm. It is known that Alzheimer's sufferers follow daily cycles in terms of irritability and irascibility. And synchronizing circadian rhythms to fit in with work and leisure patterns would greatly enhance an individual's capabilities and efficiency.

The biological clock

As long ago as 1729, Jacques d'Ortous investigated the daily cycle of the common mimosa plant. He was interested whether the plant opened and closed its leaves daily in response to the changes in the light levels or because it had an internal clock that monitored time. He put a plant in a cupboard for a few days to find out. Although it was in complete darkness and had no light cues, the plant continued to unfold its leaves in the morning and close them in the evening.

The simple experiment strongly suggested that there was an internal timer which kept track of the 24 hour cycle. When humans took part in an analogous experiment, only this time in deep caves with a light continuously on rather than in the dark, they also showed the presence of an internal clock. The existence of this internal clock was demonstrated in a charming experiment in 1955 using bees. Forty Parisian bees, trained to search for honey at a given time of day, were flown to New York. The bees continued their honey-gathering sorties on Paris time – some six hours ahead of New York time.[11]

The human internal clock runs at about twenty-five hours rather than twenty-four. So after a fortnight, the internal clock would be about twelve hours out compared to the outside world, as happened to the cave experimenters. This is where the internal sundial enters. Each morning the clock is resynchronized by the light from the rising sun. The change from dark to light is the visual cue. Blind people tend to sleep badly because they cannot use light cues to resynchronize their internal clocks.[12] While there are other cues in the environment such as temperature and the earth's magnetic field, light is by far the most important.

Using micro-surgical techniques to selectively destroy small portions of the brain in rats, early research pointed to the hypothalamus as the location of the biological clock. This is a primitive part of the brain involved in basic drives such as hunger and thirst. In 1972 scientists narrowed down the human biological clock to two tiny clumps of several thousand cells in the hypothalamus known as the suprachiasmatic nuclei (SCN). The name comes from the location of the SCN, just above where the broad optic nerve trunks cross over each other (a site known as the 'optic chiasm') on their way back from the eyes to the visual centre of the brain. It is behind the eyes in the middle of the forehead and led Michael Young, in his book *The Metronomic Society*, to compare it with the Third Eye of Buddhism, 'which is supposed to open in enlightenment'.[13]

The SCN also receives information about light and dark from the eyes, but it has its own dedicated pathway of nerves, the retinohypothalamic tract (RHT), which is separate from the main nerve bundles carrying visual information to the brain. Nerve fibres also carry signals from the SCN to the pineal gland, which affects hormones and other functions.

The SCN was identified as a biological clock because when it is destroyed in an experimental animal by pinpoint surgical lesions of the brain, rhythms in sleep and wake, and many other rhythms, fade away. Interestingly, the animal, minus its SCN, runs, eats and drinks the same total amount each 24 hours, but these activities are now randomly distributed throughout the day and night.

Why do we sleep?

A rat prevented from sleeping will lose the ability to maintain body heat and die of no apparent cause in about three weeks. As most parents of young children know, sleep deprivation is a form of torture that rapidly saps the ability to think and perform cognitive tasks. There is a rare human condition in which the sufferer loses the ability to sleep and dies in a matter of months.

It seems that humans need to sleep but the question is why? Also, we seem to require a certain amount of sleep to function optimally. A third question is whether we need to get our daily sleep ration all in one go or whether we can take it as a series of naps?

After all, cutting down on sleep would be the easiest way to solve the time shortage. There is some evidence that this has been happening. One study has suggested that contemporary American students sleep two hours less a night than their counterparts at the turn of the century.[14] But too little sleep causes its own problems.

Nobody has any very good reason as to why we need to sleep. Our hunter-gatherer ancestors in the African savannah probably had to be active during the day because they had to see what they were doing.[15] Gathering berries, nuts and roots by day when it was light was much easier as humans have relatively poor nocturnal vision – or at least modern humans have. If early humans had a poor sense of smell and inadequate nocturnal vision then returning to the family cave with a bunch of poisonous berries was not a recipe for evolutionary survival. Likewise, hunting was a daytime pursuit for humans who were more likely to be the hunted at night.

That does not explain why we sleep, only why our early ancestors may have stayed in at night. They could have conserved energy by resting without the need to actually lose consciousness and fall asleep. Daniel Dennett, director of a Centre for Cognitive Studies, solves the problem to his own satisfaction when he suggests that sleep does not need a 'clear, biological function'.[16] He turns the question upside down and suggests that it is being awake that demands explanation. According to Dennett, 'a life of sleep is as good a life as any and in many regards better, certainly cheaper, than most.' Dennett deliberately overstates his point, and for humans sleep would seem to be maladaptive. One of the distinguishing characteristics of human beings and the key to their evolutionary success is the capacity to learn. Although generations of children have believed that learning can occur osmotically by putting the answers under their pillow the night before an examination, there is no good evidence that this is how it happens. Being awake imparts a cost in terms of energy usage but it does have a certain educational value.

Sleep is presumed to benefit the brain perhaps by giving neurones a chance to recuperate. The frenetic neuronal activity during rapid eye movement (REM) sleep that punctuates our nights suggest we doze to consolidate memories. Francis Crick, co-discoverer with James Watson of the double-helix structure of DNA, put forward the idea that when we dream, mental junk is being eliminated. According to Crick we sleep to forget. However, it has been suggested that the rapid eye movements are merely a way of stirring the vitreous humour in the eye, so ensuring that a reasonable supply of oxygen reaches the cornea during sleep.

Recent work suggests that sleep is linked to the immune system. Sleep-deprived rats have high numbers of bacterial pathogens that are normally suppressed by the immune system.[17] In humans, even moderate sleep deprivation has a detectable influence on immune system cells. The immune system seems to affect sleep in return. Infections are well known to cause sleepiness and it has been shown that several cytokines, molecules that regulate immune response, can by themselves induce slumber. Cytokines have a direct effect on neural development and in rats, at least, it has been demonstrated that a gene for one cytokine becomes more active in the brain during sleep.[18] It is known that no damage to the brain prevents sleep indefinitely, so sleep must involve a benefit to neural functioning. While it is still speculation, the idea has been put forward that cytokine activity during sleep reconditions the synapses, the junctions between the neurons, thereby solidifying memories.[19] Linking sleep with the immune system offers a plausible evolutionary pathway for sleep in humans. A positive feedback loop may be involved between cytokine production, sleep and memory which could result in survival advantages. Improvements in memory and consequently in learning capacity and what we would call experience would be of benefit to early humans.

Whatever the reasons, missing even one night's sleep causes problems. In the USA 47 per cent of workers experienced at least one episode of sleeplessness in the previous three months.[20] Two-thirds of those who had trouble sleeping say they had a harder time getting through the day as a result.

The familiar culprits of stress, anxiety and worry contribute to most long nights spent staring at the ceiling: 48 per cent of sleepless workers blame stress and anxiety. But aches and pains may also be a factor. Although they do not report pain as the main reason for sleeplessness, 42 per cent of workers say their inability to sleep was accompanied by physical discomfort.

Workers who have trouble sleeping experience it on a fairly regular basis, an average of eight times per month. And there are indications that the trouble is more severe when the workday is near. On a typical work night, 49 per cent of people with sleep problems sleep six or fewer hours. On weekends, the share drops to 30 per cent.

A rough night can wreak havoc at work the next day: 63 per cent of workers who have trouble sleeping find it harder to handle stress on the job, and 60 per cent say they have difficulty concentrating. More than half find it hard to listen or solve problems. When asked to quantify these problems, people say that after a sleepless night their concentration is only 70 per cent of normal, they accomplish about 76 per cent of what they usually can do, and the quality of their work reaches only 80 per cent of normal. This opinion of the bad effects of sleeplessness carries over to others who do not get enough rest. More than eight in ten people believe that their co-workers' problem-solving, concentration and ability to handle stress decline when they do not get enough sleep. [21]

How much sleep do we need?

The multiple sleep latency test is a simple scientific measure of whether someone is getting enough sleep. All it does is see how long someone takes to fall asleep in a darkened, quiet room at 10 a.m. and then at two-hour intervals throughout the day.

Anyone staying awake at 10 a.m. for twenty minutes is alert and scores 20. A person who falls asleep after five minutes gets a score of 5. The scores are averaged over the day. Repeated testing has found that people getting eight or more hours sleep per night find it almost impossible to fall asleep during the day; those on around seven hours score about 12, i.e. they fall asleep in twelve minutes, and those on four hours or less fall asleep in three minutes, equivalent to a diagnosis of narcolepsy, the involuntary sleep disorder.

Stanley Coren, one of the doyens of sleep research and author of *The Sleep Theives*, is convinced that we are sleep deprived. He believes we may need to sleep 9.5 to 10 hours a night for optimal performance, which would put the dampener on moves towards a 24 Hour Society. Coren is supported by other

American sleep researchers, who say that the 7.5 hours of sleep that most of us manage is inadequate. A century ago people slept longer and the fact that most of us seem to enjoy a lie-in suggests that we need more sleep than we get.[22]

Dr Mark Dyken of the University of Iowa considers that we need between 7 and 9 hours of sleep a night. 'When people skimp on sleep they lose the ability to perform simple motor tasks', he explains. 'They also forget details and lose concentration skills. Sleep loss also causes irritability, depression and indigestion, and it amplifies interpersonal conflicts – all detriments to a productive work-day.' Sleep deprivation leads to a reduced vocabulary, leading to stilted conversations, shorter sentences and a greater use of clichés.

This view that we need more sleep is challenged by other sleep researchers, who liken over-sleeping to over-eating or drinking. 'We may like to stay in bed or eat a lot, [but] we don't have to. Those who sleep a little less tend to be more positive about life and mentally active.'[23]

Political leaders like to convey the idea that they manage with hardly any sleep. President John F. Kennedy is supposed to have had little sleep and likewise Napoleon and Winston Churchill. When she was Prime Minster, Margaret Thatcher claimed to get by on about four hours' sleep per night. In her case, it was part of her general image as a hard-driven believer in the Puritan work ethic. Sleep was for wimps. As Chancellor of the Exchequer, Gordon Brown is portrayed in the same terms as a dour son of the manse who burns the candle late while he struggles alone with the burden of balancing the nation's books. The Prime Minister, Tony Blair, goes out of his way to cultivate a more laid-back approach. William Hague, the Leader of the Opposition, is another politician who gets by on four hours sleep a night, in his case helped by two twenty-minute meditation sessions during the day.

Robin Cook, the Foreign Secretary, might like to compare his work habits with this 1831 diary entry by Lord Palmerston.

> My day was not an idle one, for having left the office only at three in the morning the night before I had, before the Cabinet at one, to write an important despatch to Vienna, to hear Czartoryski's account of the whole Polish War and to discuss with Cluptede all the squabbles of the German Diet. After a Cabinet, I had to see van der Weyer, Lieven, Bulow,

Esterhazy and Wessemberg upon various different subjects and afterwards
to send off messages with despatches and private letters to Vienna, Berlin,
Paris and Brussels. However, I contrived to get it all done by about two
this morning – and now for my consolation, I have staring me in the face
thirteen boxes full of papers which ought to be read forthwith and which
have come to me since yesterday morning.

Palmerston used to work so late into the night that to prevent himself
nodding off he had a special desk built so that he could work standing up.

Stalin, the dictator of the former Soviet Union, was projected as the Little
Father, a benign patriarch working for the good of his people. He claimed to
work late and said that his office lights could be seen well into the night as
he grappled with the task of improving the welfare of the people. In truth,
Stalin was often at home in a drink-induced sleep.

Stalin was not alone in feeding the image of sleep as one of indulgence.
There is probably no predetermined amount of sleep we need, beyond a bio-
logically set minimum. Even the optimal amount may vary considerably
between individuals and that still begs the question as to what is meant by
optimal. There may well be a trade between the amount of time we sleep and
the daily requirements for alertness. This will vary throughout the day and
will be task-dependent. Driving a car requires a different level of alertness
from pushing a trolley round a supermarket. Perhaps we should heed the
advice of one sleep researcher who says 'it is much more effective to take a
ten minute nap than lie in for an extra hour or two in the morning.'[24]

The idea that there can be a set amount of sleep is relatively modern and
came about as a consequence of industrialization. 'In the Middle Ages, there
was little discipline about the length of time that people slept. People were
often depicted as sleeping in the daytime and any place that was convenient,
under a tree, in a corner or wherever.'[25]

Sleep was a public event. Even nobles slept in the living chambers and
servants often settled down literally at the feet of their masters and mis-
tresses. Agricultural workers, which meant most people, would simply lie
down in the field when they felt tired and needed to sleep. Sleep did not
become a separate event with its own special times, rituals and reserved
spaces until industrialization, when work was separated from home:

Sleep has now become part of the economy, as in 'dormitory suburbs'; hotels and hospitals do their accounting on the basis of beds. The hospitality and hotel industry uses bed nights as a measure of occupancy, as do nursing homes. Where we sleep is now a major economic activity.

Physiological sleep studies have consistently viewed sleep as something completely individual, overlooking the increasing social disciplining of the sleeping–waking cycle; even the sleeping pill is partly to be understood in terms of the pressure to sleep at a socially appropriate time.[26]

Do we need to have all our sleep at once?

The World Napping Organization's purpose in life is to promote the idea that taking a nap is good for you. As the organization points out, look up 'nap' in a thesaurus and there is a rush of negative connotations: 'idle', 'remiss', 'sloth', 'indolence', 'inactivity', 'loaf', 'procrastinate', 'lethargy', 'slouch', 'vegetate', 'fritter', 'piddle', 'languish', 'inert', 'flagging'.

A restorative brief nap, the organization suggests, is the natural quick-fix for tiredness and it is becoming a regular feature of the workplace. A Tokyo company called the Napping Shop visits companies, erects tents and provides earplugs and eye masks so workers can snooze on breaks. This idea seems to be catching on with companies establishing 'sleep rooms' so that employees can take short naps to refresh themselves. Tired executives at Gould, Evans, Gould, a huge architectural practice in Kansas City, are encouraged to nap in the 'Spent Tent', where they are provided with clean sheets, a pillow and an alarm clock.[27] To accommodate travellers for whom the conventions of diurnal rhythm have become impracticable, the Hilton hotel chain offers 'Sleep-Tight Rooms' with circadian light boxes, special soundproofing and other features designed to induce restful sleep at unlikely hours.

In *The Sleep Thieves*, Professor Coren recounts how Leonardo da Vinci is supposed to have slept for fifteen minutes of every four hours so as to give himself time to do all the things he did. This spartan regime, which adds up to only one and a half hour's sleep a night, was attempted by a 30-year-old modern-day Roman actor, Giancarlo Sbragia. He tried it for six months. Initially, Sbragia claimed to enjoy the experience but after a few months he said he felt psychologically wrecked, 'I was suffering a kind of imaginative damage.' After going back to sleeping eight hours a night he recovered his dreams and seems to have had no lasting ill-effects. Other researchers have experimented with a four-hour rest/work schedule that included twenty-five minutes' sleep in every four-hour period. This was tried for two months and it seems that some people at least can manage on such a schedule for that period.

Research on napping has come to the following conclusions:

- Napping can lead to improved performance but the effects are not dramatic.
- Naps lasting fifteen to sixty minutes increase alertness, but napping an additional hour has no effect.
- The value of naps is affected by their timing in relation to the circadian cycle. A nap at 8 p.m. may help the night-shift worker on a subsequent shift but interfere with subsequent nocturnal sleep in a day worker.
- Sudden wakening from a nap is followed by decreased performance. This is known as sleep inertia and lasts for about half an hour after wakening.[28]

Leonardo probably slept normally most of the time and occasionally, when under pressure, resorted to his tough, napping regime. Despite their boasts of surviving on little sleep, Churchill was famous for taking a nap in the afternoon and Kennedy, an assiduous image-maker, may well have embroidered his sleeping habits to project signs of toughness. Whether we could manage with say one five-hour sleeping session and a nap of a further one and a half hours in any twenty-four hours for long periods of time is unknown. The possibility of manipulating our internal clocks to do that is one of the prospects offered by the research.

Manipulating the biological clock

Melatonin, called 'the hormone of the night' in some promotional literature, is an amino acid derivative secreted by the pineal gland during the night. In the 1960s, Richard Wurtman performed pioneering work at Massachusetts Institute of Technology (MIT) on the effects of light and darkness on the secretion of melatonin by the pineal. Subsequent research by Wurtman and many others has allowed scientists to trace the 'wiring' of the complex circadian system. The pineal itself is controlled by a cluster of nerve cells located just above the optic chiasm in the hypothalamus, the suprachiasmatic nuclei (SCN), that contains the circadian pacemaker.

Each night the SCN communicates with the pineal gland to stimulate melatonin secretion. Melatonin, in turn, induces sleep. The timing mechanism in the SCN itself is controlled by sunlight that enters the retina and reaches the SCN via the retinohypothalamic pathway. Thus, it is the solar cycle that drives circadian cycles – a process called 'entrainment' – and regulates the rhythms of rest and activity, and of a large number of physiological and endocrine functions. Cutting the retinohypothalamic tract abolishes entrainment, but not vision or the reflex response to light. Cutting the optic tracts abolishes vision and light reflex, but not circadian entrainment.

In 1994, Wurtman and his co-workers at the MIT reported the results of a sleep laboratory study involving twenty subjects with normal sleep habits. Subjects were administered melatonin in low doses (1–10 mg) or placebo, and sleep was monitored in the lab during five eight-hour test sessions. Compared with placebo, melatonin (all doses) decreased the time it took to fall asleep, and increased sleep duration. The MIT investigators concluded that melatonin may be as effective a hypnotic as the benzodiazepines, the best known of which is Valium.[29]

This study started a melatonin hype. Synthetic versions of the hormone were touted as being not only a wonder drug for sleep problems, but also a cure for insomnia and jet lag; it slowed ageing; it could help fight disease and improve sexual activity. What more could be asked from a drug? In Britain, travellers from the USA were asked to bring back supplies of the unlicensed drug, even though there was no labelling for dosage and side-effects, no controls for purity, and self-medicating with an unregulated product is generally a big mistake.

Lost in the commercial activity was the real possibility that current scientific research can provide the means to manipulate the biological clock and our sleep–waking cycles. Some researchers, like those from Enlightened Technologies, are doing it with light-based therapies. Others are opening up the possibility that we may one day be able to take a pill to reset the body clock for shift work or travelling across time zones.

One researcher in New York believes that the suprachsiasmatic nucleus can communicate with the pineal and other areas of the brain by chemical as opposed to neural means. One experiment showed that if all the neural connections to the SCN are cut, the clock continues to function and control activity rhythms. This strongly suggests that a currently unknown chemical, not a nerve connection, controls the body's responses to light and dark.[30]

The lack of daylight in the long winter months and subsequent depression among the populace is blamed for the high incidence of suicide and alcoholism recorded in northern Russia and Scandinavia. In Finland 15 per cent of the population claim to be affected. In Britain, many thousands also suffer from SAD (Seasonal Affective Disorder) and the treatment is to spend hours sitting in front of artificial bright light.

In what sounds more like the script for a James Bond film, a Russian spacecraft company, Energia, plans to put groups of satellites in orbit, each of which will reflect sunlight down onto northern cities from 210 foot diameter mirrors. While designed initially to help those suffering from SAD, if the project works the possibility of artificially lighting all the world's cities at night would become a reality.[31]

In our genes

The detailed way in which the internal biological clock works is emerging. It is a fascinating picture of sophisticated mechanisms controlled by two genes. Working mainly with the fruit fly, geneticists have discovered that the fly's rhythm is set by the action of two proteins, PER and TIM, made by the period (per) and timeless (tim) genes, respectively. Scientists discovered per in 1971, while tim was identified in 1994. Similar genes were found in mammals in 1997.

The fly's circadian cycle begins around noon when the per and tim genes transcribe their DNA into RNA, but only after sunset does the accumulated RNA prompt the cell to stockpile the PER and TIM proteins. At night, the proteins pair and migrate into the nucleus, home to cells' genetic material. About four hours before dawn, the level of PER/TIM protein complexes peaks, which signals the per and tim genes to stop making RNA and, hence, the protein complexes. Near dawn, the PER/TIM protein complexes disintegrate. With the complexes depleted, the per and tim genes begin to make

RNA again by midday. The rise and fall in the concentration of the proteins establishes a self-regulating cycle that is the internal timing of the body.

The scientists found that the TIM and PER proteins need each other to get into the nucleus. However, if flies are exposed to light, one of the proteins, TIM, rapidly degrades, which blocks the movement of the remaining protein to the nucleus. 'In the natural environment, even though RNA levels have been rising since midday, sunlight keeps TIM protein from accumulating until nightfall. This postponement delays the binding and nuclear activity of the PER and TIM proteins until the night part of the cycle.'[32]

This increasingly detailed understanding at the genetic level, admittedly of fruit flies, is beginning to be applied to human behaviour. By increasing the number of discrete exposures to light, the human biological clock can be shifted by up to twelve hours – in effect advancing the body's time from noon to midnight. And it is possible to get the clock, in essence, to stop altogether.

The idea of safely manipulating our internal clocks and rhythms so that we can choose how much sleep we want, when we want it, and arrange the sleep–wake cycle in such a way that our body's physical and cognitive performance peaks on demand is still the stuff of science fiction. But scientists are getting closer. A team of scientists in Chicago have found a mammalian clock gene in mice.[33] This means that understanding of the circadian rhythms in humans should be much closer and with that understanding will come the ability to manipulate them.

The field of chronobiology is very young. In less than thirty years a vast amount has been learnt about the way the body regulates itself. It is probable that thirty years from now we will have the capacity to design our own cycles for a given set of needs. For example, actors performing in the evening and filming in the day may well adjust their rhythms to hit peak capabilities between 9 a.m. and 1 p.m. in the morning, 2 p.m. and 5 p.m., and 7 p.m. and 11 p.m. This will allow for a four-hour sleep programmed in from 3 a.m. until 7 a.m., a nap from 1.30 p.m. until 2 p.m. and a further nap from 5.30 p.m. until 6 p.m. The programming would be done by setting a wrist-watch that also serves to deliver a cocktail of chemicals through the skin and into the blood at specific intervals. If the actors change their schedules then they would reset the programme to suit their new activities.

Others to benefit would include footballers in the four yearly World Cup.

To meet global TV schedules, the players turn out for some games at 2.30 p.m. local time and others do not kick-off until 9 p.m. An out-of-sorts performance by a player in these games may be due more to circadian rhythms than anything else.

Once we can control our rhythms many of the objections to shift working and to the 24 Hour Society will fall away. Until then, other means will have to be found to ensure that the advantages that come from the flexibility of a 24 Hour Society are not achieved by the exploitation of the health and safety of groups in the population.

8 Larks or owls

The prolongation of the working day beyond the limits of the natural day, into the night, acts only as a palliative. It quenches only in a slight degree the vampire thirst for the living blood of labour. To appropriate labour during 24 hours of the day, is, therefore, the inherent tendency of capitalist production. But as it is physically impossible to exploit the same individual labour power constantly during the night as well as the day, to overcome this physical hindrance, an alternative becomes necessary between those workpeople whose powers are exhausted by day and those who are used up at night.[1]

Karl Marx, *Das Kapital*

Night-working has always had a bad press. Even if he went somewhat over the top in his castigation, Marx was only following in the tradition of Victorian reformers such as William Guy, whose tract on working conditions in a bakery was sub-titled, 'Evils of night work'. But if more people are going to be working evenings and nights in the 24 Hour Society, the issues and difficulties have to be faced.

Marx was writing in the middle of the nineteenth century, when the consequences and horrors of the Industrial Revolution were apparent. Working eighty hours a week without rest days or public holidays was not uncommon. It was not surprising that one of the first demands of the slowly developing labour movement in the second half of the nineteenth century was for a reduction in working hours. This was backed by legislation restricting working hours for women and children and both moves led to a reduced supply of labour and an increase in wages. To maintain the same level of capital utilization of machinery, employers had to introduce two- and three-shift systems as a means of maintaining long operating hours.

The need to work expensive capital equipment to its limit has returned with a vengeance. Investment decisions are made on a global basis and plant operating hours and use of capital equipment are important factors. Modern machinery becomes obsolete before it wears out so it is vital that machinery use is maximized. If plant A operates 168 hours a week while plant B works only 50 hours, plant A will have unit capital costs about one-third those of plant B. This, rather than lower labour costs, is more significant in the debate about international competitiveness in manufacturing.

When Vauxhall introduced a third shift for the production of the Astra car at its Ellesmere Port plant near Liverpool, it was because it had convinced its parent company, General Motors, that it could operate efficiently over a 24 hour period.

In continuous 'never put out the fire' process industries such as oil refining, steel production and chemicals manufacturing, intensive capital utilization has long been the norm. In Britain more people overall worked nights earlier in the twentieth century, particularly in the mills, mines and factories, than do today. Evening and night-time working has been common for many years in hospitals, transport, communications, computer operations and service industries such as bars and restaurants.

What is new is that the need to work extended or non-conventional hours is pushing into many sectors that previously were unused to them. 'Whereas thirty years ago, night workers would have been exclusively in heavy or service industries, today they are increasingly knowledge and information workers.'[2] Banks used to close at 3.30 p.m. Now the high street branches open a little longer but a telephone-based banking sector is open around the clock. One in five banks is open 24 hours 365 days a year. Telephone call centres are among the fastest growing sectors in the UK economy. The call centre industry employed 1 per cent of the UK workforce in 1998. The industry is growing at approximately 40 per cent per annum and it is likely that 2 per cent of the workforce will be employed in call centres by the year 2000.

In Britain, at any given time of night, about 350,000 people are at paid work. A further 100,000 will be travelling, most of them to and from their workplace. BBC Radio 5's *Up All Night* programme has an audience of about 250,000. No one knows how many people work regularly at night as the complex pattern of shift working makes it almost impossible to avoid double-counting.

Some people for example work twelve-hour night shifts for three days and then have four days off before doing a stretch of day shifts. Others work split shifts and others a rotating triple shift. Time-use surveys report that 8 million people are still awake at midnight, 1 million of whom are working. By 2 a.m. this has fallen to 2 million and by 4 a.m. there are just over 1 million people awake. Official data from the Employment Department suggest that at the very least a little over 1.5 million people work at some time of the night. Given that some daytime employees will occasionally work into the evening and night, it can be estimated that up to 4 million people work in the late evening or during the night over the course of a year.

Of those working in the evening and at night, many will be at a second job. In 1984, 323,000 women and 378,000 men had more than one job. By spring 1997 the number of women with second jobs had climbed by 115 per cent to 696,000, while men with second jobs increased by 44 per cent to 543,000. The trend towards women taking second jobs is clearly shown in a 1997 Royal College of Nursing survey: 26 per cent of nurses said they had a second job – mainly nursing – a rise from 17 per cent in 1992.[3]

Around the world the number of night-workers is increasing. In the USA, which is in many ways leading the way into the 24 hour world, some 20 million people regularly work at night. An analysis of the 1991 US Census suggests that around one-third (32 per cent) of full-time workers have jobs on a fixed schedule of daylight hours on weekdays.[4] The Australian Bureau of Statistics estimates that about 20 per cent of the workforce is on shift rosters, and the number is increasing. The national chief executive of the Australian Chamber of Manufacturers, Allan Handberg, says that shift work will become increasingly common as economic imperatives force companies into round-the-clock production.

In future, millions more people will have to work at non-conventional times to satisfy the demand for goods and services at times dictated by the customer's wants rather than when the supplier is prepared to provide. The 24 hour availability of services such as banking, fitness centres or cafeterias also seems to improve the morale of those who work nights. Fresh Provisions, a 24 hour food store in Perth, Western Australia, reports that a considerable percentage of its custom is from shift workers who call in on the way home.

But night-work is not without its difficulties.

The problems of night-work

As many of the world's filmgoers know, the first distress call from the *Titanic* went out at 12.15 a.m. local time. Fewer are aware that the nuclear accident at Three Mile Island began at 4 a.m., Chernobyl at 1.23 a.m. and the explosion at the Union Carbide plant in Bhopal, India, at 12.15 a.m. Shortly after midnight on 24 March 1989 the T/V *Exxon Valdez* ran aground on Bligh Reef in Prince William Sound, Alaska, spilling almost 11 million gallons of North Slope Crude oil. The *Estonia* sank in less than twenty minutes in the Baltic Sea at 1.50 a.m. on 28 September 1994 with the loss of 852 people.

It is true to an extent that the big disasters seem to happen at night. But how much can be blamed on fatigue or messed-up circadian rhythms? If a boat is going to hit an iceberg, it is likely to be at night when the iceberg cannot be seen. If a group of nuclear plant technicians at Chernobyl who have been on duty for thirteen hours start making a series of poor judgements, they are more likely to do it at night rather than during the busy day. The result of that was damage of about £200 billion and the deaths of several hundred people.

The *Exxon Valdez* disaster happened at night, but not because the captain had been drinking, as is often supposed. He was not on duty at the time of the accident. The problem seems to have been a shift change that occurred just before the accident. The lookout was helping the harbour pilot get off the boat and an inexperienced third mate was at the helm. The cause of the accident was not simply tiredness but a combination of poor shift-work scheduling, human error, excessive overtime, crew fatigue, inappropriate sleep schedules, inadequate shift changes, alcohol, insufficient training, and reduced crew sizes.[5] That all resulted in over 10 million gallons of oil spilling over 1,300 square miles.

Fatigue or slow responses were partially responsible for all the above incidents and there is no getting away from the fact that night-work can be a problem. Those who work at night perform less well and make more errors. In Britain, sleep-related workplace accidents cost at least £114 million a year. The risk of injury on the night shift is over 20 per cent higher than on the day shift.[6] The key NASA officials involved in the *Challenger* disaster made the decision to go ahead after working for 24 hours straight and having had only two to three hours' sleep the night before. Their error of judgement cost the lives of seven astronauts and nearly killed the US space programme.[7]

Here are some of the major rhythmic changes in human physiology and behaviour:

Function	Day	Night
Body temperature	High	Low
Cortisol (hormone also known as hydrocortisone)	High	Low
Urine production	High	Low
Catecholamines (hormones e.g. adrenalin)	High	Low
Melatonin (sleep-regulating hormone)	Low	High
Growth hormone	Low	High
Capacity to digest fats	High	Low
Glucose levels	High	Low
Activity levels	High	Low
Blood pressure	High	Low
Sleep	Low	High
Concentration	High	Low
Memory	High	Low
Attention lapse	Low	High[8]

There is a considerable body of evidence describing the effect of these changes. Night-workers can suffer from higher levels of indigestion, ulcers, diabetes and ischaemic heart disease, quite probably resulting from eating inappropriate and difficult-to-digest meals during the night. Researchers in the USA report that 59 per cent of night-shift workers say they fall asleep at work on a regular basis. They have even coined the phrase 'blue-collar jetlag' or simply 'shift-lag' to describe the feeling of night-workers who lose a full eight hours of sleep over a week. While the Japanese have a word, *karoshi*, for overwork, a western acronym TATT (tired all the time) seems best suited to describe the effects of working changing shift patterns. The International Confederation of Chemical, Energy, Mine and General Workers Unions (ICEM), representing some 20 million workers, says that tiredness does not just affect a person's ability to work but is responsible for emotional stress at home.

A night shift is generally defined as working between 11 p.m. and 6 a.m. Shift-lag intensifies at 3 a.m. This is when the body is at its lowest ebb –

traditionally the time that nuns pray for the rest of us. So if you are awake – and demanding that the body be fully functioning by working – there is an inherent conflict occurring. This conflict causes circadian dysrhythmia, or disruption to the sleep–wake cycle. On rotating shifts it is best to work days, then evening and then nights. A different combination can make shift-lag worse.

Many shift workers never fully recover from shift work. Even if the shift work schedule is an easy one, like two nights on and five days off, the worker has less quality sleep throughout. Some take sleeping pills but many report that it does not fix the problem of lack of quality sleep.

Going without sleep for twenty-eight hours has a similar effect on work performance as a blood-alcohol content of 0.096 – nearly double the UK drink-drive limit. Australian researchers have found that 50 per cent of night-shift workers stay up the day before they begin their work, and are awake for twenty-eight hours by the time they finish their shift. Levels of fatigue on subsequent shifts can be even higher.

Dehydration is also a problem for shift workers. Drinking plenty of non-alcoholic and non-caffeine drinks will help the dehydration during the night. But it also creates a powerful urge to urinate during the first sleep after working the shift. It is a difficult choice. Fixing one problem creates another.

An Australian company, No-Shift-Lag, which markets 'natural' remedies to combat the effects of shift-lag, surveyed a night-shift workforce and produced an extensive range of mental and physical symptoms.

Mental symptoms
Partners of shift workers notice that they become more irritable after working night shifts. The survey found that relationships were more likely to break up with shift workers and the major causes cited were irritability or being 'cranky', and days of bad moods. 'Snapping or losing it' was another symptom, followed by tears. Trying to comfort shift workers under stress only added to the problem and then created difficulties for management.

Night-shift workers had an increased level of stress that made them sensitive and defensive. For example the slightest criticism would be perceived as esteem-destroying and led to disputes over small details or as one manager put it 'getting all worked up over nothing'. Some workers were so stressed with night-shift work that they became easily upset and were prone to see problems that were not really there. When asked to do certain tasks, they would frequently do something different and then argue that they were right and that management had a problem. These workers required a great deal of management time to calm them down and try to point out their contrary behaviour.

Omitting to clock in or out and forgetting to do quality checks are two examples found in the survey. Many small tasks, done automatically during the day, were forgotten at night and the impact of all these combined to cause major problems.

Physical symptoms
Workers complained of being worn out and tired for days after night shifts, generally accompanied by a lack of concentration and motivation, especially for any activity that required effort or skill. Even simple daily activities became harder.

Shift workers in the survey reported a lack of energy in all the normal activities they used to enjoy before working night shifts, such as gardening, home maintenance and recreational sports. Their sex drive also dropped, but since it does for most people as they get older this may or may not be attributable to shift work.

Working between midnight and 5 a.m. disrupts circadian rhythms and this can cause the night-worker to wake during the next sleep and then want to fall asleep during the next shift. Once the inbuilt circadian rhythms have been disturbed it can take several days for the body to readjust. Broken sleep stops the shift worker getting quality sleep which delays any recovery from shift-lag.

Increased constipation and fluid retention were reported by night-shift workers in the survey. Other studies into shift work have reported similar findings. An increase in stomach problems was also reported. But some of the problems were attributed to night-shift workers not eating properly. Of course, a night-shift worker who has an upset stomach may not be keen on eating.

The survey of night-shift workers reported a greater number of sick days being taken because of colds, coughs, sore throats and flu than among workers who did not work nights.

Morning people and evening people

Some people are natural day workers and others seem to prefer the night. Some people leap out of bed at the start of a new day ready to face the world, while others drink endless cups of coffee to get going and do not really come alive until later in the day. The world is divided into morning and evening people, into larks and owls. A 1997 survey showed 42 per cent of British adults consider themselves to be larks and 34 per cent say they are owls, the remaining 24 per cent claim no real preference.[9]

Ageing seems to turn us into larks: more than half of those over 65 say they are morning people, against only 22 per cent of young people under 24. It will be no surprise to parents of children in their late teens and early twenties to hear that 60 per cent of that group consider themselves to be evening people. And whether it is the fresh air or the dawn chorus, 58 per cent of adults in rural areas classify themselves as larks and only 31 per cent in the inner cities.

People are either larks or owls because all human biological clocks do not run at the same speed. While light is used as a reference point each day to reset our clocks there are other signals that affect the internal ticking. This was first discovered in the 1930s when an American doctor, Hudson Hoagland, was looking after his wife, who was ill with flu. Hoagland was a trained physiologist and he noticed that when he left his wife for a few minutes she complained that he had been gone for a long time. So he asked her to count to 60 in seconds and checked her temperature while he kept an eye on his watch.

Hoagland found that the higher his wife's temperature was, the faster she counted so that her minute was only 38 seconds. He concluded that the heat made her internal clock run faster. Studies on sub-aqua divers whose body temperatures were lowered in cold water show that in those conditions the internal timer runs more slowly.[10]

One way of determining peak performance time is by taking a person's temperature regularly over 24 hours. The period of greatest alertness is generally when the body temperature is rising to its peak. Some people who are natural larks find evening and night-time working extremely difficult because that is when their internal timing is slow and they should probably avoid it. The large numbers of people who like working nights have a different biological clock. Mark Norris, owner of Insomnia, a Glasgow all-night café, has no difficulty recruiting staff to work at night. 'Doing the graveyard shift suits some people. Just as some customers find it convenient to eat or buy food in the middle of the night, there are a lot of people who prefer to work these hours.'[11]

It has also been established that introverts seem to be larks, performing many tasks best in the morning, while extroverts do the same tasks best in the afternoon.[12] Older people also tend to find evening and night-work hard, but most individuals who cannot tolerate late hours of work have usually stopped by their forties. Older night-workers have usually adapted their domestic arrangements so that they have support systems to cope with their work schedules.

THE MATHEMATICIAN

Mathematicians are not like other people. Paul Erdos, who died in 1997 aged 83, was distinctly odd. He was celibate all his life and home-less for most of it; his worldly possessions fitted easily into two battered suitcases. He would journey from one mathematician's home to another and work with them on problems in number theory. It was life stripped down to its owner's bare essentials. Despite having no family or social responsibilities, Erdos had a problem with time. To get the work done he slept only three hours a night.

Working at night is not uncommon among mathematicians. Profes-sor David Singmaster prefers to start work after dinner. He is a retired professor of recreational mathematics and though he says that mathe-maticians, including himself, are fairly normal it has to be said that there are not that many men in their late fifties whose studies are filled with Rubik's Cubes and hundreds of other puzzles and games. He claims that it is the logicians who are distinctly odd.

Singmaster prefers the night because it is quiet. 'Newton was once asked how he made his discoveries. By thinking about them all the time was his reply.' Like many mathematicians and scientists who are owls, Singmaster finds it easier to think at night. He goes to bed between midnight and 3 a.m. most nights. David Deutsch, the leading

British quantum theorist, works at night, as does Leon Feigenbaum, one of the founders of chaos theory. John Conway, an Irishman of original mathematical genius, is believed by his colleagues not to sleep at all.

How to cope with night-work

Considerable research conducted over the years has suggested ways of lessening the effects of late evening and night working. Unfortunately, few companies and organizations have taken the time and trouble to inform their employees of the practical steps they can take, some of which are outlined below. All too few implement working schedules that reduce the potential harmful effects from disrupting the sleep–wake cycle.

- It is important for night-workers to manage their sleep during the day, not only the length of their sleep, but also its soundness. This is made easier by relaxing without caffeine, sleeping pills, alcohol or nicotine before going to bed. All distractions such as phone calls and lights should be screened out. Ideally, the night-worker should go to bed at the same time every day, and the temperature in the room should be cool – around 20°C. Noise especially is the great enemy of day sleep. Using foam ear plugs, insulating the bedroom with heavy drapes and carpets, and muffling noises with a fan or 'white noise' machine all help.
- It is advisable for employees to be prudent about volunteering for overtime, double shifts or short callbacks. An occasional 'emergency' at work is one thing, but working a double shift almost every night requires a complete change in lifestyle. Those who do work mainly at night have to accept that their daytime routines will be different. It is unwise to try to lead a 'normal' life during the day and then work an evening or night shift as well. Planning social events and family outings can be a challenge, but it's not impossible.
- On days off, overlapping half the usual work period with sleep will prevent a shock to the body rhythms on returning to work. For example, if the usual shift is midnight to 8 a.m, the night-worker should stay awake till 4 a.m, then sleep till noon.

- Sleeping in two four-hour periods right before and after the shift is the best way of coping with a temporary night-shift.
- Because of the way the body's digestive system behaves, the best advice is to eat lightly and healthily at night. Extra energy should be obtained from vegetables, cereal, rice, pasta, fruits and juices. Sweets and fats are best avoided or at least cut back. If possible, food should be eaten as several smaller meals rather than one or two large ones. Toward the end of the shift it is best to avoid eating at all. Night-shift workers complain about putting on weight. Some take dumb-bells to the workplace and exercise during the breaks.
- It is important to take all the permitted breaks during the night and because the body's performance is not as efficient as it is during the day, extra care should be taken with all procedures. Most night-shift workers drive home from the workplace. There are more road accidents at night than there should be compared with the accident rate during the day, even allowing for the increase in traffic.
- The biological need for sleep cannot simply be ignored. All night-shift workers should take their only nap of the day of at least thirty minutes just before going to work. After the shift, it is best to go to bed as soon as possible rather than stay up for hours.

Shift schedule

There are many biological and social problems associated with circadian-unfriendly rotating shifts, namely a week on days, followed by a week on nights and then a week on afternoons/evenings. Physical problems include an incidence of peptic ulcer disease eight times that of the normal population. Cardiovascular mortality has also been noted to be increased among shift workers. It is estimated that the risk of working rotating shifts is close to smoking a pack of cigarettes per day.[13] Other physical problems include chronic fatigue, excessive sleepiness and difficulty in sleeping. Part of the social toll on those who must work rotating shifts is reflected in an increased divorce rate. Shift workers are also known to have higher rates of substance abuse and depression and are much more likely to view their jobs as extremely stressful.

The best thing from a circadian perspective is to work a long string of nights, say four to six weeks. The idea is that individuals can group their nights for the year together and have to shift their circadian rhythms only twice, once onto nights and once back again. Everyone will work hard for that one period, but have ten to eleven months of the year when they will work only an occasional night, on special cover. It is important for the night-workers to stay up even on their nights off so as not to lose their hard-won adaptation.

The worst is the zombie schedule, such as working fourteen out of fifteen days, sixteen-hour shifts, unpredictable and excessive overtime, or counter-clockwise rotations.[14]

The strategy often used in Europe is to work as few a number of nights in a row as possible, ideally one. The idea is never to shift the circadian rhythms but to maintain a constant diurnal orientation. Working four to seven night shifts in a row is universally condemned. The body suffers from inappropriate phasing during each night shift and then just when the body starts to adapt to nights, it switches back again, experiencing the worst of both systems.

A wide variety of stimulants and relaxants have been tried by those working shifts but in nearly all cases they have either little or no effect or else have unfortunate side-effects. Sedative hypnotics, for example, are very addictive if routinely used and while they do increase total sleep time during the day, they do not hasten resetting of rhythms to night shifts or improve alertness during the night. Caffeine can increase alertness and is nearly universally used by shift workers but it should not be used within four hours of a planned sleep period. Alcohol induces sleep but of poor quality. Alcohol-induced sleep is markedly distorted with little of the deep REM sleep which has been shown to be vital for well-being. Daytime sleep contains less REM sleep than at night so it is important that the REM content is not further diminished.

Astronauts face peculiar time-shift difficulties. When orbiting the earth every ninety minutes, they experience eighteen sunrises every 24 hours. The interior of the spacecraft is kept very bright and the astronauts receive doses of bright light and melatonin. A great deal has been learnt from the space flights and the speed with which chronobiology is advancing makes it likely that it will soon be possible to rapidly adjust circadian rhythms using combinations of light and drugs. If that possibility is realized then workers will be able to safely adjust their rhythms to match the working conditions.

The classic all-night workplace is the operations or control room of a process industry such as a nuclear plant. This is really a 'monitoring' room where the operator sits in front of a group of computer screens waiting to respond to an alarm. Operators seldom get up and move around the room, as they are simply waiting for a problem to occur. Monotony can very easily set in. Compounding the problem, the rooms housing the control systems are typically kept dim in order to enhance computer screen visibility, and darkness promotes sleep.

For the most part, the equipment maintains the process efficiently within preset parameters. However, it is possible for the process to stray outside the parameters, and this is when human interaction is paramount in averting disaster. It is at this point the operators need to be at peak alertness, able to respond quickly and with mental acuity. It is difficult to snap instantly from semi-somnolence to peak alertness and this is a major problem.

A possible solution

ShiftWork Systems (SWS), a US-based company that also works in Europe, designs and manufactures a circadian lighting system (CLS) that is tailored to the employees. SWS has installed CLS in control rooms, quality control labs and supervisors' offices in both nuclear and fossil fuel electric utilities, chemical processing plants, oil refineries, manufacturing environments, hospital clinical settings, and at the Nuclear Regulatory Commissions Headquarters Operations Center. The NASA Space Flight Medicine Department has been using SWS technology since 1990 to preadjust shuttle astronauts to varying launch times or split-shift crews. 'What we do, very simply, is we fill a room with light,' says Ted Baker, ShiftWork's president. 'Depending on whether a particular employee is working a first night shift or a third night shift, depending on when their shift turnovers occur, and depending on what the crew structure is, the software is calculating an optimal lighting regimen for each and every work shift.'

This blast of light begins gradually, as any sudden changes in luminance are uncomfortable to the eye. Under computer control, the fluorescent fixtures gradually begin to 'ramp up', that is, the amount of light they emit increases. In a matter of twenty or thirty minutes, the light in the room intensifies, almost imperceptibly, from a standard office level of about 150 lux to around 8,000 lux, similar to dawn or dusk. (Bright daylight is about 100,000 lux.) If workers are vigilant about sleeping in a very dark room during the day (to avoid counteracting the night-time treatments), within two days their circadian rhythms and sleep schedules are synchronized with their workday.

At present, these systems are used in large industrial control rooms and military installations. Companies like ShiftWork Systems and Enlightened Technologies are working on portable versions that will enable individuals to shift their circadian patterns to meet different needs. When that happens we will be able to trade day for night at will.

9 Competing on time

From now on the world will be split between the fast and the slow

Alvin Toffler, *Powershift*[1]

In the opening sequences of the American film *Jerry Maguire* (1996), the Tom Cruise character decides to write a new and more ethical strategic direction for the sports agency he works for. He writes feverishly into the night and then goes to an all-night copy shop to get his *cri de cœur* copied, bound and delivered to his colleagues by 9 a.m. Unfortunately for this example of the 24 Hour Society and round-the-clock opening in action, he gets fired for his temerity.

Richard Branson probably saw the film and, never one to be backward about riding a new trend, his Virgin Group has taken a 50 per cent stake in the British and French developments of Kinko's, a US-based chain with over nine hundred business support service centres in nine countries. The company has opened two stores in central London and plans to have about a hundred in the UK by 2004, providing 365 days a year, round-the-clock office services support to all sizes of business from one person freelances to large corporates.

Kinko's demonstrates how a time-driven society and the growing need for instantaneous communication is determining the way in which business operates: 24 hour opening is a response to customer demand. Real people as well as Jerry Maguire want to use the service in the middle of the night. These can be individuals getting party invitations done, students preparing a thesis or consultants smartening up a report through to small businesses and large corporates. The company's main business is to provide small and medium-corporates, from law firms to multinationals, with an outsourced service that meets all its printing and information needs. Apart from copying, binding and duplicating, the full range of services includes video conferencing, Internet access, scanning, and electronic transmission of documents. Printing businesses have traditionally worked overnight; what is new is the addition of a full digital service and extending it into a retail offer. Kinko's shops are not the familiar high street copy shops. Each Kinko's is at least 5,000 square feet and is full of the latest digital printing, scanning and copying machines.

The key issue is not that the Kinko's shops are open all night. It is that the company has recognized that the successful supplier is one who can profitably meet customer demands whatever they are and whenever they are made. Customers now expect their demands to be met at a time of their choosing. If that happens to be in the middle of the night or first thing in the morning, then so be it. Many British businesses are still working to a time pattern set long before the Second World War, which bears no relationship to the way the world is now operating.

People have become used to saving time through the purchase of convenience foods and microwave ovens; they also know about value for time, namely that an experience that uses up time should be a worthwhile experience and provide them with value for the time they have given up. Now they are learning about the third of the time criteria, 'time choice', or having the freedom to choose when to do something.

The current preliminary commercial moves to a 24 Hour Society are concerned with customers' freedom to choose when they want something. The prioritization of 'time choice' means that businesses have to rethink their hours of access. It is not enough to be open all hours; what is required is being open and operating at what the customer wants. A shop that is open all the time, but has little stock on the shelves in the late evening, misses the point. The smart companies also appreciate that the quality of access is as important. The customer waiting area in a Kinko's is a pleasant, well-fitted space where drinks are available, not a scruffy chair in the corner of the shop.

Kinko's understands that increased competitive pressure has sharpened what has always been a point of difference between companies, namely time, into a strategic issue. Time appears in the business world in many guises: time to market, down-time, real time, customer-facing time, fee-earning time, on-time. Some companies recognize that these terms are part of a business shift from economies of scale to economies of time. It is the speed and responsiveness of an organization that now gives it a comparative advantage. FedEx, which is in fierce competition with other global courier companies, builds time into its whole raison d'être. Their company statement is: 'We will deliver the parcel by 10.30 a.m tomorrow.'

But this time competitiveness has to be embedded in a deeper context of being a customer-led organization. It is no longer good enough to have the right product at the right price. It also has to be at the right place and at the right time. All four factors have to be present to satisfy customers. This changes the rules of the game.

Companies are no longer in control. The customer now directs the operation, not the supplier. In a 24 Hour Society, the customer at least has the chance of being king. Faced with customers who are in a hurry, businesses must compete not only on cost, quality, technological innovation and overall service, but also on time. Time separates the market leaders from the market failures.

This shift of focus is occurring throughout the business world. Software companies now offer a fax-back service for customer queries. Using a keypad phone, the customer selects the query from a menu and receives a fax detailing information on the query. This is now being applied to all manner of product information across a wide range of sectors.

A generation ago, camera film was processed via the chemist or by mail and the prints returned anything from three to five days later. Today new processing machines enable specialist shops to process colour film in half an hour. Digital technology has produced cameras that take instant pictures for viewing either on the camera's own screen or later on a PC. By the year 2000, these cameras will be sold with their own photo-quality dedicated printers, directly challenging the dominance of conventional film.

In the USA, a Washington company Let's Eat Already offers a home meal replacement service. The company sends cooks to the customers' homes to prepare a freezer-full of dinners. Another enterprise, Kids in Motion, chauffeurs children to and from music lessons and soccer games while Script 'n' Scribble sends gift parcels to the children while they are at holiday camp, complete with a personalized note.[2]

Viking is a prime example of a company who has understood the importance of time in business, especially small businesses. The company sells office stationery to the 'SoHo' (small office–home office) market. Although the Viking main catalogue carries over 10,000 lines, orders phoned in before 11 a.m. will be delivered the same day virtually anywhere in the UK. Order after 11 a.m. and the goods arrive the following day.

Viking knows that customers do not want to spend time ordering office stationery, so the whole process is made as trouble and time free as possible. It has taken to heart the maxim, 'Customers use our time up until their decision to buy, after that we are using their time. Therefore we must deliver immediately.'[3] The company answers the telephone before the third ring, every time. There is none of the 'All our operators are busy at the moment. Please hold.' Viking knows the call pattern into its offices and how many operators it needs to handle the volume of traffic so that the telephone can be answered before the third ring.

Companies such as Viking understand that for customers it is the total time of the encounter that matters. Just as customers become frustrated enough to leave a supermarket when the check-out queues are longer than seven people, so they get angry if they have to spend five minutes hanging on the telephone for a one-minute transaction. Similarly, the speed of transaction was at the heart of McDonald's success as it rose to market prominence on the promise of the ninety-second hamburger. Business customers' demands for the self-service check-out in hotels led to budget hotels where customers let themselves in by swiping a credit card and leave in the same manner. There is not even a time-consuming human interaction. It all saves the customer time.

Convenience, product quality and price are exemplified by McDonald's, Viking and budget hotels. To go further and participate in a 24 Hour Society needs the addition of time choice. This is the promise offered by the Internet.

The growth of the Internet
It is impossible to overstate the significance of the Internet and the way it creates new time patterns. The total value of goods and services traded over the Internet in 1997 was less than £6 billion. This is expected to double every year until 2002, so a reasonable estimate for the total value traded then is close to £200 billion. There were 130 web-sites in June 1993. In 1999 there

are over 1 million. In the USA, over 70 million people use the Internet, 6 million are on-line in the UK and the global total is well over 100 million. A teenager working from a bedroom in Cheshire can launch a web-site and within 24 hours be taking orders from Turku to Tuscon. There has never been anything like it.

The Internet releases customers from time constraints. They can view the web-sites at a time that suits them, decide on a purchase and by inputting the relevant credit card information confirm the purchase instantaneously. The site carries information on stock availability and delivery, consequently customers know when they will be receiving the item if it is a tangible good. Intangibles, such as financial services, airline reservations and educational material can be bought, confirmed and downloaded in a matter of moments. Improvements in the Internet itself combined with the falling cost of the telephone links will drive large sections of retail and intermediary business onto the Net and end the tyranny of opening hours.

The Internet meets the three customer time criteria. It saves time by speeding up the process of product and service selection and purchase. It can provide value for time if the web-sites are designed to entertain as well as inform. And the Net obviously meets the criteria for time choice as it leaves the customer to decide when to go shopping on the Net.

Amazon is a well-known example of what is happening in this new Internet economy. Since 1996 Amazon.com has sold books to 3 million people in 160 countries by providing the three customer time criteria. In a shrewd move, Jeff Bezos, the company's founder, established an on-line front-end book ordering system and placed it next to an established US book distribution centre. Amazon does not hold any stock in its Seattle offices. It processes the orders that come in over the Internet and passes them to the book distributors. In this way, customers all over the world can browse a 3 million book and CD catalogue and order any time they choose any day or night of the year.

To provide value for time, the Amazon site offers book reviews, special offers as well as directing the customer to books on the same subject they are interested in. The site not only offers value for money, even if the book is delivered outside the USA, but also genuinely provides value for time by helping the customer and both informs and entertains.

So what happens to the high street bookshop? It adopts a new persona. A bookshop is no longer a place for simply buying a book. It is a place to browse, get advice, meet other people, have a meal, listen to music and even sit and read. New bookshops, such as the 30,000 square foot Waterstone's shop in Glasgow with over 150,000 titles, are a new type of store. They open early for breakfast and close late. There is a coffee shop in-store where people can meet and a Café Internet cyber café for the web surfers.

This is happening to all forms of shopping. Retail bank branches almost became redundant some years ago when the cashpoint first came into existence. If most of the branch outlets were not on extended self-repairing leases, the main banks would have drastically cut the number years ago. Attempts to justify this property-driven approach and its restrictive 9.30 a.m. to 3.30 p.m. opening hours were made on the basis that face-to-face banking was necessary even for routine transactions. First Direct, a subsidiary of the Midland Bank, realized there was an opportunity for a branchless bank in 1989 when it introduced 24 hour telephone banking. At the time, the Internet, or rather its predecessor, was used only by the military and computer nerds. The telephone, however, was familiar and for banking purposes could handle most of the things customers wanted. First Direct and its many competitors soon learned that while banking is necessary, banks are not.

Since 1989, First Direct has built a customer base of over 850,000. Very few people call in the middle of the night to check their bank balances. Calls start to come in around 6 a.m. and peak between 10 a.m. and noon. But about a quarter of total calls are made between 5 p.m. and 10 p.m. and around 4 per cent of all calls are made in the hour before midnight.

By 2002, various predictions suggest that up to 9 million people in Britain will be using the Internet to handle their personal banking, superseding the telephone in the process.[4] And what will become of the bank branches? They will be turned into late-closing restaurants and coffee shops.

The Internet is fine for ordering and intangibles can be delivered electronically, but tangible goods still have to be physically delivered. FedEx was probably the first company to realize that a global delivery service, operating around the clock, would give other businesses the flexibility to operate when they wanted to. Through this insight a giant industry was born.

FedEx

Nicholas Negroponte is Director of the MIT Media Lab in Cambridge, Massachusetts, and the recognized seer of the Information Age. He uses laptops like other people use a watch and travels the world advising organizations on what is going to happen in the Brave New World dominated by bits rather than atoms, or information rather than manufacturing.

While he is an unusual human being he is still human. He sweats like everyone else. As a result his shirts get dirty. When he is travelling abroad on long trips, Negroponte sends himself clean shirts from home by FedEx and sends the dirty ones back by the same means. Negroponte uses FedEx as a travelling wardrobe in the same way as many companies use it as a mobile warehouse. Instead of carrying inventory, companies are discovering that their goods can be continually on the move from factory to final customer without having to spend expensive, revenue-eating time in warehouses and in transit sheds. Because FedEx works round the clock, goods can be on the move 24 hours a day, providing a global web that enables a factory in Singapore to be supplied on a just-in-time basis with components from one in Ohio.

On the back of this offer, FedEx has built a business. The statistics are impressive on any count. Each day, 140,000 FedEx employees deliver over 3 million packages world-wide. To get them to the customer, the company's 40,000 vehicles cover more than 2.5 million miles. FedEx is huge. Its 600 plane fleet is larger than any commercial airline and most of the world's air forces. Thirty-two call centres around the world handle 400,000 voice calls a day. Over 50 million electronic transmissions are processed daily. All this to get the package there by 10.30 the next morning.

FedEx is a company built on time. Its corporate literature is studded with phrases such as 'time-definite delivery commitment', 'real-time tracking', 'time-sensitive'. Time, time, time. The company is so time conscious that its planes have the slogan 'The World on Time' painted on the fuselage. Time is the essence of the company. At its Memphis SuperHub a giant clock counts down the seconds every night as the incoming parcels are sorted for onward dispatch. On a smaller scale, FedEx's British operation at Stansted works to a careful schedule that unloads, loads up and turns round the daily incoming plane from Memphis in a little over two hours. Customers can track the passage of a parcel to its destination in real time by the use of FedEx software. Customers can log on to the system and check for themselves where the parcel is at that precise moment. That is instantaneous customer service that collapses time to virtually zero. This is what it means to compete on time.

FedEx's beginnings are legendary in the business world. Frederick Smith, the company's founder, wrote a paper while a student in the mid-1960s at Yale, on the need for a new 'hub and spoke' air courier delivery system. Smith saw that the changing economy would need an efficient system to move high priority, time-sensitive packages. He was marked average for the paper, put it aside and (unusually for the offspring of a wealthy family) went and flew fighters in Vietnam. Back home in Arkansas in the 1970s, Smith approached the Little Rock airport management to help him build an air courier business. He was turned down and instead went to Memphis. Smith put up $4 million of family money with $80 million of venture capital to launch Federal Express (as it then was) on 17 April 1973. On the company's first night in business, fourteen FedEx jets took off from Memphis with just 186 packages. Not too auspicious a beginning, but the business idea, involving as it did a challenge to the placid monopoly of the US postal service, was strong enough to create a new industry.

The rest as they say is history, although it has taken FedEx a long time to make real money. FedEx created an industry by exploiting the time elasticity of price. They first promised to deliver a package or letter by 12 noon the next day, then they offered delivery by 10.30 a.m. the next day. Before FedEx the typical customer had to wait at least two days or longer for delivery. Customers soon learned the value of the offer.

Monte Face, managing director of FedEx operations in Europe, has been with the company since 1980, so he is in a good position to judge if it has changed.

> It is basically the same company. We move packages from here to there. But it has grown and developed its own systems. It is a business that never stops. Seconds count here more than in any other. In order for the planes to hit their time slots everything has to happen on time. We have to hit the ramp on time, hit the hub on time, hit the courier system on time.

National Semiconductors is an example of a company that has rethought its distribution system in order to compete on time. At the start of the 1990s the company took fourteen days to deliver the products from the factory to the customer. Now delivery happens in two days. The company closed or downsized nine distribution centres and reduced its logistics staff by 500; it has switched all its distribution over to FedEx.

Small companies can now offer round-the-clock service by plugging into the global distribution offered by courier firms such as FedEx. In the USA, FedEx introduced a Sunday delivery service in March 1998. This enabled a small business such as Micky's Minis Flora Express to develop a seven day a week, 24 hour national service. The company specializes in small potted plants and counts supermarkets, convenience stores and hardware shops among its customers as well as garden centres. Delivering throughout the seven days ensures that the company gets its plants to the stores in good condition and minimizes wastage.

FedEx and other companies that work round-the-clock have created what is essentially an Internet for shipping and distribution. This network is more than just an instrument for sending something from here to there. The new systems take away the disadvantages of size and geography and global expertise. Companies can offer their products in the certain knowledge that they can be delivered thousands of miles and several time zones away literally overnight. This allows even small companies to operate globally. A specialist clock-maker or a bookseller, for instance, can receive orders around the clock from anywhere in the world via the Internet and send the product to just about anywhere in the world via an air courier. Working globally in this way means that companies run on world time rather than local time.

FedEx and other delivery companies are service companies in the sense that they have no definable product. But they are now totally integrated into the manufacturing and logistics systems of major and minor global companies. FedEx is an example of the power of a network that increases in value as the number of end-points grows. By putting the World on Time they have the effect of changing the view of time to a 24 hour CanDo world.

Tesco

Tesco is a company that has learned the optional freedom that comes from a reliable logistics system. By becoming as adept at its own internal distribution as FedEx is on a global basis, the company has established a competitive advantage in the tough UK supermarket business.

Since the passing of the Shops Act 1994, it has been common for super-markets to open all night Friday and for several nights in the run-up to Christmas. In late summer 1998, Tesco shocked its rivals in the British super-market business by announcing that with immediate effect 63 of its 588 stores would open all night every night from Monday through to Saturday. These stores would close only Saturday night and Sunday night.

A week later, Tesco announced that it was going to expand its chain of fif-teen late opening Tesco Express convenience stores through a tie-in with Esso the petrol retailer. The aim is to have a hundred Tesco Express stores on petrol forecourts by the year 2002.

The scope of this 24 hour expansion far outstripped its competitors. Yet as Ray Jackson, manager of the flagship Tesco Brent Cross store in north London explains, 'At a stroke we increased our business by about 10 per cent. We would have to add on several thousand square feet to do that another way.' Colonizing the night is good business for Tesco. The reason its com-petitors do not follow suit is rooted in decisions taken in the mid-1980s.

Selling food is much like delivering parcels. It is relatively simple once the logistical systems are in place. A systems-driven business still has to hit its time points but as long as it does it can be sure that it will deliver what is needed when the customer wants it. If stores are going to be open round the clock then it is imperative that the shelves are fully stocked. The customer will forgive the absence of the odd exotic produce, but there is little point in shopping at midnight if there is no milk or bread on sale.

Tesco knew that it could keep its shelves stocked because it had spent more than ten years establishing industry leadership in distribution. The key decisions and the associated investment were taken in the early to mid-1980s. Before then, each store was responsible for its own ordering and stocking. Some supplies would come from one of the store's warehouses but suppliers would also arrange their own deliveries and it was not uncommon to find the streets around a store clogged with supplier vans and trucks. In the bigger shops there could be up to fifty trucks delivering every day. The net result was that one item in ten was usually out of stock and not on display. The only way to improve the stock position was to devote space in the stores to warehousing rather than to selling space and to hold buffer supplies: both were costly and wasteful.

Tesco's radical solution was to centralize all ordering and stocking. Nine warehouses served all the stores in Britain. Orders came into a central unit from the stores via the electronic tills and on the basis of customer demand and company experience, suppliers were informed, again electronically, of the company's needs. Deliveries to each store were cut to two days and suppliers were given thirty-minute time slots to deliver into the warehouses. In many ways this mimicked the FedEx 'hub and spoke' operation.

The results of this revitalized delivery system were that between 1983 and 1993 Tesco reduced out-of-stock items to 1 per cent, increased the turnover of its stock threefold, reduced the order-to-delivery cycle from 128 to 24 hours and shipped ten times as many cases of produce as sales increased. The company now operates with about 30 per cent less inventory than its nearest competitor.[5] This advantage counts for a lot.

If the distribution systems are in place then the mechanics and costs of all night opening are straightforward. A large 35 check-out supermarket will have about 450 staff in all, including part-timers, and a turnover approaching £100 million a year. About 45 people will be working nights anyway on cleaning, maintenance, shelf-filling and taking in deliveries. The stores are heated and lit at night so the only extra cost is the till staff.

In the Brent Cross store, Ray Jackson knows that there is a reasonable amount of trade until midnight and that it tails off after that. From about 2.30 a.m. there is little business until 6 a.m. so one check-out till is enough. But it is not just the extra trade that makes opening through the night worthwhile.

> It changes the way we do our business. I used to think in terms of the store opening and closing. That was the day done. Now I think in terms of a continuous process, in a circular way if you like. It means that you are always thinking ahead. The staff seem to like it and we have no difficulty getting people to work late. Apart from the premium we pay, they say that it is less stressful at night. There is less hassle and time to talk to the customers. The customers also seem to like it. There is none of the aggravation of trying to hustle them out of the store that happens when a store

closes at 10 p.m. They can take as much time as they want. And because it is easier to travel late in the evening or early in the morning by car we get people from all over north London and extending up the motorway into Hertfordshire.

Several other benefits come with 24 hour opening. The stock is turned over even faster, so is it fresher. Cleaning is a continuous activity so the stores are cleaner and tidier. Bank and building society cashpoints are inside the store, providing a far safer environment for withdrawing cash than doing so late at night on a dark, deserted high street. Jackson believes that being open 24 hours keeps management on its toes and that all the processes seem to work better.

Tesco and the other supermarket groups are experimenting with home delivery service. The customer will be able to order by telephone, fax or Internet and either collect a made-up order from a store or have it delivered direct to the home or workplace. While delivery hours will be restricted, probably to between 9 a.m. and 7 p.m., ordering will be possible at any time.

Home delivery is one of the black holes in the commercial moves towards a 24 hour world. Some delivery companies are beginning to extend their times into the early evening and appliance manufacturers are now willing to offer morning, afternoon or evening delivery slots. But all too often, the only sign of the attempt to deliver a parcel is a card, 'Sorry you were out when we called.' More could be done to ensure that deliveries arrive when people are at home. Apart from telephoning before calling in person, more delivery companies could modify their hours. One survey suggests that early evening in the week would be the most popular time for home deliveries, though 50 per cent of the population would be happy to take deliveries on a Saturday or Sunday.[6]

24 hour services

Dry cleaners, hairdressers, share-dealers and every other supplier is going to have to learn that customers want their services outside conventional hours. Just as Kinko's learned that business customers decide when they want to be served, so companies and individuals who provide personal and other services are realizing that to keep a profitable business they must be open when the customer wants.

THE BARBER

Dennis Reynolds understands what customers want, though his business is not quite in the same league as FedEx, Waterstone's and Tesco. His two-chair barber shop in Brixton is on the upper floor of what can only be described as a fairly dilapidated two-storey warehouse. A TV is on in one corner, a sound system booms out of the other. The bare walls are covered with signed photos of boxers and examples of Dennis's art, like a BMW logo carved out of the hair on a young man's scalp or a Mike Tyson style crop.

If you want a haircut at night then Dennis Reynolds is your man. He runs London's only all-night barber and it is also one of the friendliest. Any time on a Friday or Saturday night, he and the other barber, Rocky, give neat trims to the dozens of men who make up the clientele. The rest of the week he closes at around 9 p.m.

Dennis Reynolds started helping out in a barber shop at the age of 11 and his certificates are in hair styling instead of business school, but he knows a trend when he sees one. 'Next door to us is a 24 hour snooker hall and over the way is a Tesco that opens until 10 p.m. every week night and through the night on Friday. There are lots of clubs opening up. Brixton is really starting to happen and there is going to be a lot more activity in the evening and at night.'

Asked if it is worth staying open so late, he replies that he has a steady stream of customers.

> There are people who work shifts, some want a trim before going on to a party, occasionally someone comes in who has a job interview in the morning and wants to look good. There are also regulars who prefer to come home from work, have a meal, watch some TV and then come and get their hair done. When I worked in my old shop with my brother, people were always pleading with us not to close just yet and give them a cut.

It is hard work but Reynolds is young and naps in one of the chairs when things are slow. He says that nobody comes in after 4 a.m. so he tends to knock off then and come in late the next day. But he has learnt one thing which is an object lesson to all other businesses. He has a different price for afternoon, evening and middle of the night displayed on a board outside the shop. A £7 cut in the afternoon shoots up to £20 at 3 a.m. It is known to the academics as the time elasticity of price. Reynolds justifies it by saying that he would rather not be working at that time, but if people want him then they have to expect to pay for it. This is sophisticated temporal pricing, something the big supermarkets are only just coming round to thinking about.

It is not yet quite the stuff of Harvard Business School case studies but Dennis Reynolds' barber shop is catching the next wave as surely as the other companies. The educational world is learning this lesson as it moves from being essentially a public good to one that is increasingly driven by market pressures. Private schools are experimenting with the length of the school day and the growth of distance learning has expanded the opportunities for 24 hour delivery of material. Britain's Open University was one of the pioneers of distance learning and since the early 1970s has built up a huge bank of programmes. These and material from other sources have been packaged together by BBC Television under the Learning Zone brand. Broadcast on BBC2 during the week between 00.30 and 7 a.m. a typical night's programmes include geology, climatology, environmental science, Greek, business studies, engineering, philosophy and history of art.

Students generally record the relevant programmes on video for viewing when convenient, but a small number do watch the programmes as they are transmitted. It is a cheap way of providing distance learning and because students can tailor their viewing to their own schedules it provides the necessary flexibility for those who have to work or have caring responsibilities. As learning becomes one of the defining characteristics of modern societies there is likely to be a huge growth in the transmission of specialist programmes during the night.

Also set to grow is round-the-clock share dealing. To date, only about 5,000 British investors use the Charles Schwab Internet site to deal in shares, compared to nearly 2 million Americans. This is likely to change when the second generation Internet site comes on-line. Investors will then be quoted a buy and sell price and will have one minute to decide what to do. Clicking a mouse button will confirm the deal. The advantage to private investors is that not only will they know the price at which they are buying and selling but dealing charges will be far lower than at present, averaging perhaps £10–15 a trade. At the moment, private investors need a return of around 5 per cent just to break even on their dealing charges. While it does not bring the private investor quite in line with the big boys who handle clients' money, it does go some of the way to making them feel like a real trader.

THE TRADER

Mike Dollar's children will not go into the same business as him. At least, not if he can help it.

It is not the job itself. Dollar is a Dallas-based high-risk futures manager, known in the trade as a short-term technical trader, and he loves it. It is just that it is such hard work. There is a market open somewhere in the Standard & Poor futures and the metals, currencies and crude oil in which he trades just about every minute in the 24 hours. It is the ultimate 24 hour business. The only break is on Saturday and part of Sunday, but even then he and most of his colleagues come in over the weekend to check trading positions and pick up on research. At least once or twice a month he gets a call at home in the middle of the night and he knows that his office is not ringing him to tell him that the market is going up. It is always bad news and at 3 a.m. he has to be up and ready to act.

It is a nerve-jangling business. Each Standard & Poor future contract is $250,000 (about £160,000), but it takes only $15,000 to trade, a leverage of eighteen to one. Which is fine when it is going in your direction, but not good at all when you get the bet wrong. As Dollar's trading partner says, 'We juggle dynamite for a living'.

Dollar accepts that successful traders have to be addicted to it and somewhat obsessive. It is not something that can be done without total commitment. Dollar, an athletic 43 year old, is in his office before 7 a.m. By 8.30 a.m. when the main markets open, he and his colleagues have gone through all the reports and determined their trading strategy. For the next nine to ten hours he stays in the room, watching the trading screens. His meals are delivered and eaten at the desk. When he leaves the office, he has a pager which is constantly updated with market information and, like most of the senior people, he has a system at home to receive quotes data.

Traders are driven by the markets and Dollar, like all traders, lives by the markets' opening and closing times. 'My family life is run on similar lines. I hate being late for anything and we are good time managers, we have to be.' A strong family man with three children, he manages only a week's holiday at a time. Even then, he stays in touch with his office daily and usually hourly. And he always comes home at least a day early, which he admits drives his wife crazy. A two or three week break is out of the question.

Mike Dollar admits that the pace gets harder as he gets older. He works out to keep himself in trim but he accepts that it is getting tougher. There is no way he can change the pace or find more time in the day because of the relentless discipline of the markets. Which is why his advice to his children and to others if they want to go into trading, is – don't.

If organizations want to compete on time, they have to learn a new culture. They have to bring time into the price, product, performance trade-off that they offer the customer. To do this requires that the organization, in the words of Jack Welch, the boss of General Electric, stops operating 'with its head towards the boss and its ass towards the customer.' Customers must know that time will no longer inhibit businesses meeting their demands.

10 The 24 hour city

24 hour cities are places where people live, work and congregate 24 hours a day. The best places to invest are where people want to be. Where people go, investors are going to follow, where people depart, investors will be on their heels. 24 hour cities have the most secure long-term investment prospects.[1]

Jonathan Miller, *Emerging Trends in Real Estate*

Manchester, Leeds, Sheffield, Birmingham, Bolton and Cardiff are among several British cities that have applied the 24 hour city sobriquet to themselves and use it as part of their marketing campaigns for investment and tourism. It is a glamorous sounding idea. Sexy even. And sex sells. In the USA, Equitable Insurance has stated that the place where investors want to put their money, the 'hot' properties of the late 1990s, are the 24 hour cities typified by San Francisco, Seattle, Boston, Chicago and New York. But is it just a property hype or is there any substance to the idea of a 24 hour city?

Is it more than simply sound city centre management, with extensive use of closed circuit TV cameras to maintain a watchful eye on the public? Does developing the night-time economy of clubs and bars add up to a 24 hour city? Is it just a case of keeping the central parts of the city alive in the twilight hours between the time when work stops and the shops shut but the 'good night-out' has yet to start?

The 24 hour city is a response to the 'hollowing out' of cities that has occurred since the late 1960s as people in full-time employment left the city centres for the suburbs and the 'new towns'. By the 1970s, the thriving city centres of the 1960s were often deserted. Central heating meant that homes became more comfortable and turned into 'cellular households'. All rooms could be used, even in winter, and combined with DIY improvements and low-cost stylish furnishings, the home was more attractive than most pubs and other leisure attractions. Twenty-one-inch colour television sets took leisure activities away from communal centres such as the cinema and the pub into the private, often suburban home. The demise of the city centre was made worse by poor planning, an unwillingness to ensure survival by changing centres to mixed-use areas, and a regulatory and policing regime that feared people enjoying themselves.

A 24 hour ethos is an attempt to regenerate these city centres. It is a process whereby towns and cities are discarding the old 9 to 5 time clock and seek to exploit the economic, social and cultural benefits of 16, 18 or 24 hour levels of activity. But it is also more than that: it encompasses the central issues in urban planning. The 24 hour city is now an accepted short-hand for the many debates on the future of urban living, urban economies, public social life and the public realm.[2]

These debates are being articulated in cities around the world. As cities try to reinvent themselves, the 24 hour city is more a collection of ideas and methods than a literal description. There are no objective rules for deciding what is and is not a 24 hour city. Nor is there a single model for developing one. Different cities use a mixture of different approaches. The particular combination depends on local circumstances and the availability of funds. In all cases, the hope is that by creating activity after normal office/shop hours a more vibrant urban culture will be developed.[3] There are many paths to the 24 hour New Jerusalem, but for analysis there are three broad categories, none of which is mutually exclusive.[4] The liveliest cities use every approach.

Urban design and public space

Successful urban design can change not only the look but also the character of a city. The best examples of this long-term, whole city approach can be seen in mainland Europe. Consistent and well-researched design and planning since the early 1960s have enabled Copenhagen to become a city of squares, cafés and streets filled with people walking, sitting, watching and being watched.[5] The city has deliberately encouraged an evening economy and increased city centre residency, matched by appropriate scale architectural design to increase the volume and quality of street life in the city. The Danish approach captures what the British architect, Richard Rogers, believes is the essence of city living, the sense of mingling with other people and being part of the space itself. The Italians call it *la passeggiata*.

In Barcelona, mayor Pascal Maragal revitalized the city through a series of major developments including staging the 1992 Olympics but more significantly by creating 150 new public squares. The city also reconnected itself with the sea by developing the defunct industrial dock area that separated it from the water. Barcelona is now characterized as an archetypal 24 hour city whose sense of excitement and fun has been a major factor in transforming it into a world-class city.

In Britain, Birmingham has pursued a long-term urban design process in an attempt to transform the city centre. In what can be described as a hard-edged physical planning process, Birmingham's large-scale investment in the central business district has succeeded in raising the city's profile and attracting business tourism. This is important in a city that has seen its manufacturing base deeply eroded since the late 1970s.

The city has built a splendid convention centre and plays host to conferences and congresses of up to 30,000 participants. In 1998 it hosted a prestigious G8 summit. But when delegates and visitors stumble out of the convention halls in the early evening they find a quiet town centre. About 80,000 people work in the centre of Birmingham, but 80 per cent of them live outside the city limits. At 5.30 p.m. they are off home. It is not quite the Philadelphia that the American comedian W.C. Fields visited and, when asked what it was like, replied 'It was closed', but vibrant is not the first word that springs to mind.

Despite considerable physical regeneration by an ambitious civic leadership, Birmingham still behaves like an industrial city, the 'workshop of the world' as it used to be known. It is a place that thinks in terms of clocking on at 8 a.m. and clocking off at 5 p.m. It expects its dinner to be waiting on the table when it gets home.

Birmingham's great rival to the claim of second city in England is somewhat ahead in making the cultural transition. Greater Manchester is home to over 100,000 students – the largest concentration of students in Europe; it is one of the gay capitals of the world; it has a thundering evening economy of bars, clubs, restaurants and entertainment and it is transforming itself from an industrial giant of the past that was at least the equal of Birmingham into a thoroughly post-modern city. A small example of what this means in action is shown on the World Wide Web. Search for the phrase '24 hour city' on Yahoo!, Lycos or one of the many other search engines and the screen is full of references to Manchester as THE 24 Hour City.

A residential population in central Manchester of well under 1,000 at the start of the 1990s, has increased ten-fold largely by enthusiastically committing public support to the idea of urban housing and strongly identifying central Manchester as a lively, 24 hour city. The housing was provided in collaboration with developers and private and public funders who together gained in confidence over the viability of the investment. The council also has a relaxed attitude to planning, allowing an eclectic approach to development that is sympathetic to a free-wheeling urban existence.

What sets Copenhagen, Barcelona, Manchester and other cities apart is that a clear, central vision was allied to a human scale of development so that the citizens could see the incremental improvements accumulating in such a way as to improve their general quality of life. This tight–loose arrangement, whereby a tightly controlled central framework is implemented by a loose variety of flexible partnerships and agreements works with the chaotic grain of cities. Street markets are a good example of such tight–loose arrangements. The overall framework of the market – the space it will occupy, the times it will open and close, the nature of the goods that will be sold and so on – is under local authority regulation but its individual working and success is down to the many interactions between the hundreds of stall-holders and the public.

Strategic plans and huge investments are necessary for large scale reinvention and regeneration on a 24 hour platform, but much can be done using careful design on a lesser scale. In Brighton, the development of the sea-front Arches is an example of an attempt to use the physical environment to create a 24 hour micro-zone. The sea-front had always been a shop window for the town's tourism and conference industries, but over the years large parts had become run down and shabby. In particular, some of the Victorian arches on the Lower Promenade between the piers had fallen into disrepair and become derelict. In a conscious redevelopment, led by the town council, over £4 million has been spent on improving the sea-front physical environment including the Lower Promenade and Arches. The money went on building a traditional timber boardwalk on the beach, creating a Fishing and an Artists' Quarter, building a mini-amphitheatre for open air perfor-mances, installing closed circuit television (CCTV) and new lighting, creat-ing a beach volley court, and installing artist-designed street furniture. Grants were also made to new and existing arch holders for renovation. The result has been to turn the area into a sophisticated and exciting meeting place that heaves with younger people on warm evenings until well into the night.

The abandoned proposal to enclose the London South Bank complex in a glass wave would also have created a 24 hour mini-zone if for no other reason than the micro-climate created would have raised the ambient tem-perature by about 3°C. The climate of the South Bank would have been sim-ilar to that in Bordeaux. If that were to be combined with external table heaters, the area would have had the potential for round-the-year, round-the-clock outdoor eating and drinking. It would have helped to integrate the complex into Southwark Council's overall schemes for improving the viabil-ity of the borough which has had considerable success, based on sound plan-ning principles.

Putting tables outside is, in many ways, the cheapest and most significant development in bringing 24 hour living to Britain's cities. It looks trivial but the growing propensity to have tables outside links the interior world of cafés and restaurants with the outside, the private with the public. It was not always so. Local authorities were reluctant to allow it happening partly because they feared tables, chairs and glasses could be used as lethal weapons, partly because of their innate conservatism.

It is only since the mid-1980s that regulations have been relaxed in some cities. Brighton has more restaurants and cafés per head than any other out-side London and the council believes that its positive encouragement gives a more continental feel to the town. Chester calls its policy of encouraging outdoor cafés 'Chester Alfresco'. The lack of 'transitional spaces' between business and street activity is one of the reasons Bolton Council has identi-fied as limiting its evening economy.[6]

The evening economy

When Ken Mackie started as Wolverhampton town centre manager in 1991 he did not have much to start with. The town had been hit badly by the economic ups and downs of the 1970s and 1980s, much of the heavy metal-bashing industry had gone and there had been race riots on the streets. The town centre was a depressing place, full of boarded-up shops.

Mackie's job was to improve the town centre by encouraging co-opera-tion between the retailers, property owners, local groups, the police, the council and anyone who had an interest. While not solely confined to boost-ing the evening economy, it was a large part of the job.

Cars were allowed back into the city centre in the evening to reduce the feeling of a desert, environmental improvements continued and a well-lit entertainment area was developed and promoted. By 1998, every Friday and Saturday night 25,000 under 25 year olds were pouring into the clubs and bars in the town centre. Many of them are among the 30,000 students in the Wolverhampton area. Late night buses policed by club bouncers take people home after the clubs have finished. About 1,500 jobs were created and whereas in 1991 there was only one late night venue open, in 1998 there were forty with 2 a.m. closing public entertainment licences. It is a remark-able regeneration given that Wolverhampton is not naturally one of the world's great entertainment cities.

Whereas Bolton is unhappy with its narrow evening economy, Wolver-hampton accepts that it has made the best of its limited options. While its evening economy is very different from the 24 hour ethos of a city where people of all ages mingle and interact within the public space, it has enabled the city to begin the regeneration process and played a large part in altering the perception and image of the town. Essentially, the Wolverhampton evening economy is about consumption, deregulation and public order.

The key feature to the evening economy is alcohol licensing. Through most of the twentieth century, British licensing authorities have been more concerned with public order than any attempt to enhance the vitality of the cities. Councillor Peter Hopson, who chairs the London Borough of Croy-don's licensing sub-committee, is one of many activists in local government who want to see the balance changed. 'The local authorities should be the licensing bodies, with the magistrates acting as an appeals body. This would allow us the scope to co-ordinate the location and regulation of enter-tainment zones within the general framework of plans for an evening econ-omy.' Peter O'Connell, Chief Whip in Lambeth, believes that the revival of

Brixton has been based on a dynamic evening economy due largely to an unplanned liberalization of the licensing activities.

This reflects a changing police view of public order issues which has had to shake off the bad urban experiences of the 1970s. In the past, the police in Manchester and many other towns invariably objected to licensing applications. But attitudes have changed and now there is close co-ordination between the various authorities to ensure that closing hours are staggered, public transport is available and that clubs and bars participate in 'responsible host' schemes designed to manage not only the entry but also the departure of customers.

Urban regeneration through stimulating the evening economy, like all aspects of regeneration, is difficult and takes time but the monetary rewards can be considerable. The evening economy of clubs, bars, restaurants, pubs and cinemas is estimated to be anything from 5 to 15 per cent of the total British economy. In Manchester it is worth over £300 million a year without including hotel takings.[7] But it is only a staging post on the way to a 24 hour city.

Cultural quarters

The north Italian city of Padua is the grandparent of the cultural quarter. Padua has one of the oldest universities in Europe and an awesome cultural heritage. It is still a lively town, crowded with young people and tourists in the evenings. The Caffe Pedrocchi, opposite the university, has been a meeting place for artists, writers and intellectuals since 1831 and until early in the twentieth century it was open 24 hours a day.

The cultural and intellectual spirit of the nineteenth-century Caffe Pedrocchi is the third approach to a 24 hour city and there are hopes that it can be found in the unlikely surroundings of Sheffield's Cultural Industries Quarter. It may not be Padua, but over 1,000 artists, musicians, film-makers and supporting businesses have turned a derelict southern part of Sheffield's city centre into a new cultural centre. In early 1999 it became home to the National Centre for Popular Music and the council intends that by 2007 the Quarter will provide over 4,000 jobs in the cultural industries. Built into the plans is the intention to create an all-seasons 24 hour zone.

The idea behind the cultural quarter in Sheffield is that arts and cultural activities can potentially revitalize industries in cities that have forever lost large parts of their manufacturing base. Of course, the work is of a totally different nature. Labour is not measured simply by the hour but by different criteria associated with taste, style and fashion. Work-groups are relatively small, made up of younger people and individual skills and abilities are differentiated by talent as well as experience.

The old time dictates of the industrial past do not count. The work can start at 11 a.m., break at 4 p.m. and continue again from 10 p.m. This creates a 24 hour demand but it does so by imposing a new temporal system on a city that has a history of rigid time-keeping. Sheffield had always been a monolithic industrial town, insular in its thinking and lacking the easy cosmopolitanism of cities that have a history of successive immigrant populations.

The development of such cultural quarters happens more readily in cities with a strong cultural tradition. The Temple Bar development in Dublin came from small-scale entrepreneurship and cultural activity in a an area of the city in which planning blight offered the framework for a low rent, 'alternative economy' to become established. A lively local cultural district was established by combining new ideas about appropriate design and the conventions of time.

The early development of Manchester's café quarters was similarly by small entrepreneurs who brought a diversity of approach to their style of doing business and the visual appearance of their shops and bars.

The problem for such quarters is that as they become successful they become commercially attractive. The big breweries move in and before long every cultural quarter looks just like any other as the assembly-line rolls out the identikit bars and themed pubs and restaurants. Instead of being a working, cultural quarter where people live and work in an area which is open at times to suit local demand, it becomes another sanitized, heritage site.

American 24 hour cities

The American model of the 24 hour city is based on reviving the downtown area, often known as the central business district, and its immediate neighbouring areas. Instead of 6 p.m. exodus from these business districts which contain the financial centres and the main retail outlets, the aim is to reinvigorate them by attracting a residential population. This is achieved through

- attractive residential neighbourhoods rooted in and around business districts
- a multidimensional environment providing cultural entertainment, restaurants, and leisure activity day and night
- convenient shopping with supermarkets, pharmacies, etc. within walking distance in addition to speciality stores
- relative safety and security
- established and reliable integrated public transport to move people in and out as well as around the city.

The successful 24 hour American cities such as San Francisco and Seattle have not just attracted residents back into the inner core. They have integrated public participation in urban planning into their electoral system.[8] Local elections are not just about choice of candidate, but also about the opportunity to make decisions about city policy. How much office space should be allowed? Which regeneration plan is best? Which transport strategy should be adopted? The inhabitants of these cities are given not just a feeling but actual measures of control over their immediate surroundings.

It is not as easy as it sounds. San Francisco and Seattle may have been able to revive their inner cores, but Atlanta and St Louis have not. It needs a raft of factors and in particular a partnership between the developers, the planners and the public to make it work.

Even then, it is not always to advantage. Despite Las Vegas' free-market and free-booting image, in many ways it is the most planned city on earth. It was built where it is for a reason – gambling – and everything else followed suit. The casinos never close and deliberately have no windows or clocks so that their clients lose track of time. Las Vegas' 24 hour economy is based almost exclusively on hotels and entertainment to service the gambling clientele. It is a model of round-the-clock living that few want to emulate, no matter how popular it might be with tourists.

Time for a change
The 1996 Department of Environment report, *Household Growth: Where Shall We Live?* put a time-bomb under every local authority in Britain. The report's main finding was that between 1991 and 2016, the UK would have

to find room for another 4.4 million households. This was 1 million more than the figures currently being used in planning.

While about half the growth in the period was projected to be due to an increase in the overall population, the other half was composed of changes in the way we live such as more divorces and later marriages. There would also be an increase in single older households as an ageing population resulted in more widows and widowers.

Even if the new projections are overstating the facts, it seems incontrovertible that more new homes are needed and the majority will have to be provided on 'brown-field' sites in cities. For two demographic groups, the 24 hour city is an attractive inducement to living in the centre of a town. Young singles seem to want the excitement and facilities of city living. They like the idea of living close to their work or college and see home, the gym, the office, the coffee shop, the supermarket and the bar more as experiences to be had each day rather than merely functional places to go. Joining them will be the empty nesters – the baby-boomers who, in their fifties, find that their children whom they raised in their suburban homes have left. If they stay in the family home they are faced with lots of maintenance, dark bedrooms and large gardens with a rusting swing.

The key to increasing large-scale residential living in city centres is the price. One way of reducing the price is to increase the supply of both private and social housing by increasing the density of residential development. Just as the night represents a time frontier to be colonized, so the space frontier can be colonized by building down into the earth and up into the sky. Most British cities are not great works of art that demand intense aesthetic preservation. They are not Florence. What is needed in city centres is a far higher density of housing, draconian reduction in availability of car parking space and the integration of home and work that follows. This would allow lively, multi-use environments to develop, some of which will add a temporal differentiation by becoming 16, 18, 20 and 24 hour zones.

Designs on time

Both US and British city centres suffer from the predominance of single-use buildings.

> Traditional city buildings in which studios sit over family homes, which sit over offices, which sit over shops, bring life to the street and reduce the need for citizens to get into their cars to meet everyday needs. But these mixed use buildings create complex tenancies which local authorities find hard to manage and developers find hard to finance and sell. Instead, private and public developers prefer single-function buildings.[9]

Developing multi-use areas is not easy. It is easier to build for single use: one tenant and the deal is done. But single-use buildings are monochronic. They are occupied between certain hours and are empty the rest of the time. At Ford Motor Company's European headquarters near Brentford in Essex, one new recruit was startled on his first day in 1968 when he realized that between 8.20 and 8.40 a.m. the escalators only went up. Likewise between 4.45 and 5 p.m. they only went down. In business districts such as the City of London, after the offices close the areas are pervaded by a 'death-like stillness'.[10] As the journalist Andrew Marr describes: 'Walk through it now and you don't find the seething, ear splitting swarm that astonished visitors in its Victorian and Edwardian heyday. The square mile of Thames clay that was for several centuries the most crowded, competitive, energetic human colony on the planet is today peopleless and bland. After hours, the City is the most mournful place in England.'[11]

In a 24 Hour Society the buildings are polychronic. People come and go at all hours to use the various residential and commercial facilities. Number One, Poultry in the heart of the City of London, by the Mansion House, is hated by the Prince of Wales. But Lord Palumbo's building is already creating an exciting and dynamic space which promises, in a small way, to be a prototype of the way forward.

The basement houses several shops, a restaurant, coffee shop and hairdresser. The ground floor, with its walk-through atrium that provides a public space, has several clothes shops. On top of the building is one of the few high-quality restaurants in the City and on the floors in between are offices. The building has a long way to go before it can be classified as 24 hour – it is not yet being used for residential purposes – but it has the 24 hour ethos and is a refreshing change to the typical stuffy buildings in its immediate environment.

Architects are beginning to change their considerations to both long- and short-term factors. It is all very well to design neo-classical monuments but this style of decorative building either works as a whole or not at all. Columns and pediments cannot be tampered with. But buildings now need temporal flexibility designed into them. Today's schools and offices may be tomorrow's living space. That is why the best new buildings look so functional. Quaint notions about building for posterity are mercifully vanishing as adaptability and change of use becomes the determining requirement from a building. What the architects have yet to learn is the possibility of building in much shorter-term changes over the course of 24 hours.

A building and a neighbourhood can change its manners over the course of a 24 hour period. The most obvious variable is lighting. At present, nearly all lighting in commercial premises is binary: it is either on or off. It does not have to be. The internal lighting level can reflect the occupancy of the building while the intensity, frequency and colour of the external lighting can incorporate a creative aesthetic designed to enhance the overall environment. The Leeds Lighting Initiative, launched in 1993, has shown how to generate interest from building owners and has led to dramatic new floodlighting schemes at some of Leeds' most prominent buildings.

Leeds' visual appearance after dark has improved significantly as lighting schemes have now become the norm in the city centre, and almost all new buildings or refurbishment projects being proposed in the area now include lighting as a matter of course. This is making a significant contribution to the efforts to stimulate interest and activity within Leeds city centre around the clock.

And why stop at lighting? 'Whole walls of buildings can be digitally flooded with sound, colour and light, images and texts flowing in endless transformations, when whole environments respond to our body movements and the articulations of our voices.'[12] Materials in buildings façades can respond selectively to light and temperature to change appearance throughout the day and night. The 24 hour city can also be the chameleon city, appearing afresh every few hours.

The focus in the 24 hour city shifts from cars to pedestrians. But traffic control need not be an all-or-nothing affair. Time-based traffic control allows car access to streets to vary over the 24 hours. Greater care needs to be taken with public transport facilities. The Buchanan Street bus station in Glasgow

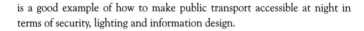

is a good example of how to make public transport accessible at night in terms of security, lighting and information design.

The compact city

Neither the British nor American examples of a 24 hour city quite fit the bill yet. In most cases, they are no more than short-term attempts to fix a problem. What is needed is a new idea of how cities should be. Richard Rogers, who is leading the British government's Urban Task Force, has expressed many of them in what he calls the 'compact city'.

In his 1995 Reith lectures, Rogers shocked many of his listeners when he described the way in which some American cities are divided between the classes. He singled out Houston, where a six mile network of underground streets has been excavated beneath the city's central business district. This underground system is entirely private and can be entered only through the lobbies of the banks and oil companies that dominate Houston: 'the car-choked streets are left to the poor and unemployed, while the wealthy workers shop and do business in air-conditioned comfort and security.' It was Winston Churchill who said, 'We make our buildings and our buildings make us' and perhaps he had a future Houston in his prescient mind.

Rogers contrasts this dystopian view of a city with the sense of community that can be gained in the great public spaces in European cities, such as the covered Galleria in Milan, the Ramblas in Barcelona and London's parks. City centre violence in New York a century ago led to Central Park being created as a safety valve where different classes and ethnic groups could mix.

Rogers' solution is the compact city: a high-density city grown around centres of social and commercial activity located at public transport nodes that provide the focal points around which neighbourhoods develop. The city is a network of these nodes or neighbourhoods. The thinking behind the scheme is predominantly spatial but it is possible to add a temporal dimension if the centres of at least some of the nodes are specialized 24 hour zones. There could be an education area based around an always-open university which could include a museum, bookshops, student accommodation, learning-related businesses – effectively a Learning Zone. A railway station could anchor the transport district and a hospital the healthcare area. Each zone would have its own complement of residential housing and local shops and services. While there will be specialization, no zone will be exclusively focused, bearing in mind the real vitality of cities lies in their diversity, architectural variety, teeming street life and human scale.

The compact city is not the same as a small city. Zones can be duplicated and put together in a variety of ways, Lego style. The idea is to bring people's homes, work and leisure into close proximity, removing their dependence on the car, and provide for a 24 Hour Society to prevent the exodus to the suburbs. The changing demographics of society and the growing numbers of the young singles and the middle-aged suggest 'the cycle of urban decline is swinging. The long night of American cities may have some way to go but it is drawing to a close. It is the suburban life-style which shows signs of fraying and over the next twenty years the older suburbs will display all the urban ills.'[13] Unlike the compact 24 hour city that maximizes interactions, the suburbs are designed to minimize human interactions. They negate the energy and dynamism of a city and draw away its vitality. They are the black holes of the urban landscape, once life enters it is trapped there forever.

Electronic communications will create an all-embracing web connecting all the elements that make up the compact city. The need for physical travel is dramatically reduced and consequently so is traffic congestion. Commuting peaks are a thing of the past as large numbers of people live closer to their work and at least part of the time work from home. Traffic flows are smoothed over a 24 hour cycle. Residents can order whatever physical goods they want whenever they want, assured of rapid delivery. A complete 24 hour world can be created without stepping outside a front door. While that might be of considerable benefit for housebound older people, it would lose the vital interactions that characterize a city.

The connected city is both liberating and imprisoning. To be able to access local government services at any time is useful but it means that the chance encounter in the post office queue disappears. Neighbours would still live next door, but neighbourliness, based on dozens of random interactions, would have to be created. It is the random interaction that gives a city its sense of excitement. Remove it carelessly and much of what makes a city work will be lost.

A mayoral agenda?

Anyone who attends a conference on urban regeneration or the future of cities soon starts to climb the wall at the incessant chanting of words such as 'vision' and 'holistic'. Trotting them out as turgid bullet points quickly kills off any belief that the local and national authorities of Britain's towns and cities will be able to deliver the dynamism and sheer panache needed to transform the metropolis into a lively, public realm.

The transformation will be difficult enough as it is. The traditional British way of life is not conducive to the experimental, chaotic desires and dangers that make city-living different from suburbia. Too many wish to recreate orderly suburbs in the centre: 'there has been much debate as to what extent Britain and the cities of northern industrial Europe ever had public spaces of sociability and how this may have been frowned on more than in the Latin countries with a strong civic tradition and hot weather.'[14] Furthermore, surveys suggest that when people are asked about housing they want traditional houses with gardens. But while there is much to be said for consultation, designing for living requires an artistic sensibility that can provide the public with an environment they did not know could exist. But of course much relies on the quality of the execution. Too many public buildings and spaces in Britain have been ruined by cost-cutting.

The 24 hour city agenda is tailor-made for a mayor. In the year 2000, London will elect Britain's first new-style mayor and the idea of a 24 hour city will play a key role in the campaigns. It will be up to the mayor to generate interest in the 24 hour city. With his or her access to public platforms and the ability to cajole, persuade and perhaps even inspire local communities, the general public, the investing sector and the various sectional interests, the mayor can enable it to happen.

11 The 24 Hour Society – solution or problem?

Old habit of mind is one of the toughest things to get away from in the world. It transmits itself like physical form and feature.

Attributed to Mark Twain

The idea of the 24 Hour Society receives a mixed response. For many of those who feel there are not enough hours in the day it is a blessing; to others who may be just as busy it as an anathema. The market research surveys show that the idea divides society – young against old; town against country; employed against unemployed. In the jargon of the marketing world, the time-poor support the idea, the time-rich are either indifferent or opposed.

Some trade unions feel that it will lead to exploitation of their members. USDAW, the main union representing shopworkers, believes that 'there is a price to be paid for greater convenience and it is our members who are paying it. We do not want to be seen as killjoys but many of our members would rather not work Sundays or through the night but have no choice because they are coerced or desperately need the money.' Other unions accept that a change to more flexible round-the-clock shift patterns may be the single best way to raise productivity. In Finland, some industries operate on four six-hour shifts and find that productivity stays around the same due to lower absenteeism. Staffordshire provides the best ambulance service in Britain in terms of response time and to do this it rosters its ambulance personnel in line with the predictable flow of 999 calls. The Confederation of British Industry (CBI) thinks that 24 hour activity can be a good thing. The TUC accepts that it is happening and should be managed so that everyone benefits.

Professor Laurie Taylor is concerned that a 24 hour society could lead to

the emergence of a new servant class who will be working night shifts to meet the demands of a new timeless and placeless elite. When huge numbers of working-class people were involved in shift-work, they did not have the economic power to demand services. But now shift workers are increasingly knowledge-workers they have more political clout and their demands for services to be adapted to their needs is being answered.

There are critics who go much further. Journalist Quentin Letts describes the 24 Hour Society as 'an Orwellian world in which offices never shut, streets are never empty and in which the cacophony of life continues unchecked from dawn to dawn.'[1] Dr Scobie, a psychologist at Glasgow University, is worried: 'we need some sort of mechanism that separates the day from the night. Night is naturally the time we sleep and we've moved away from that.'

But people do not find the lifestyles that they are leading today easy. *Homo mundialis modernicus* are wearing themselves out meeting the time demands of the modern world. 'One cannot meet the growing demands of modern social life, fill out the necessary forms, plan the children's schedules, keep the household running, except at the cost of temporal gymnastics especially exhausting for the nerves of the working woman.'[2]

Juliet Schor castigates the pace of the modern world.

On the one hand we see a higher level of stress and burn out – people are overloaded. Secondly we get a premium on the value of time outside of work, an acceleration of daily life and an increasing demand for convenience and consumer goods. We get fast and pre-prepared food, we have mail order shopping, we have automated tellers and in America where these things are extremely well-advanced we even have drive through church services, or what we might call McGod.[3]

The 24 Hour Society could offer a solution to the time-squeeze. Or it could lead to a privileged few enjoying levels of service at the expense of an overworked majority. Criticisms fall into two categories: those who are against the principle of a 24 Hour Society, and those against the practice.

There is a third category of those who are against it in both principle and practice.

In the beginning

> And God saw the light, that it was good; and God divided the light from the darkness. And God called the light day and the darkness He called night. And the evening and the morning were the first day.

The debate is not new. The division between night and day occurs in the fourth line of the Bible's book of Genesis. It is as deep as anything in the human psyche. Attempts to turn night into day and to beat time also go back a long way. Herodotus tells the story of an Egyptian king for whom an oracle had predicted death in six years: 'perceiving his doom was fixed, he had lamps lighted every day at eventime… and enjoyed himself turning the nights into days and so living twelve years in the space of six.'[4]

The religious objections are based on the idea that there is a temporal order, determined by God. Men and women should live by this celestial rhythm that includes Sunday as a day of rest and the night as the province of the dangerous and the profane. The night is seen as a boundary and crossing it is by definition to transgress. The night is a time of forbidden pleasures exemplified in the red light districts that come to life when the sun goes down. It is also a time of fear. Bad things happen at night.

Associated with this religious objection to extending into the night is the British attachment to a pastoral vision of the world. Cities are seen as artificial environments where people are up all night while rural folk are sound asleep in their beds. This cultural objection is not shared in other European countries, many of whom have just as strong a pastoral tradition as Britain. All this spills over into the environmentalist argument that seeks to reduce consumption, opposes hedonism and sees the 24 Hour Society as being profligate in its use of resources and unnecessary in terms of its rewards.

There is a strong Puritanical undercurrent in all of these objection to the principle of a 24 Hour Society. It is a moral posture that identifies consumption as wrong and even sinful. It has a long pedigree. There were sumptuary laws as far back as the Middle Ages and in the 1760s English law still required that no man shall be served more than two courses at dinner while 'France drew the legal line at three'.[5] Theologians, philosophers and environmentalists have long disapproved of the desire to consume that lies behind the demands for a 24 Hour Society. Many of them ascribe to the idea that if only we could consume less, we could work fewer hours, consequently there would be no need for shops to be open at extended times as everyone would have all the time in the world.

It is hard not to snipe at the elitism behind the anti-consumer approach. There are legitimate grounds to berate the excesses of packaging and the externalities of pollution, exploitation and congestion. But it does seem that the call for reduction comes mainly from those who have a comfortable lifestyle. Consumption may have transcended desire to become an end in itself, but rightly or wrongly consumption is the way in which those who consume pursue happiness. Maybe their time would be better spent in self-improvement by reading a book, growing vegetables or learning a skill. But as Lord Grade often said, 'Give them what they want'. Those who oppose the 24 Hour Society in principle should try explaining to the shoppers at Middlebrook how their lives were somehow better under the rigid time constraints of a generation ago.

Striking a balance

The 1960s decade was not simply a cultural revolution in terms of sexual and social mores, but marked the beginning of the slow decline of the deferential society in which the 'great and good' determined the way in which ordinary folk would live their lives. This included both the nature and the timing of pleasures. It was a time for throwing off constraints. The decade also inaugurated a profound change in the relationship between home and work with the beginnings of the end of the classic nuclear family. It is hard to believe now that at the start of the 1960s, there were quotas at universities for the percentage of women in certain courses and most professions were almost exclusively male. As women started to enter the workplace in increasing numbers and levels of seniority so the home has increasingly become more like hard work. When both parents work, home is a place of deadlines and time discipline. It is ruled by schedules imposed by the fixed times set by schools, shops and services. Work is now often seen as an escape, a place of relative calm. It is where most people make their social contacts and many feel that their workplace 'family', a feeling encouraged by organizations, is in many ways more rewarding than their real one.

It is this change that is causing problems with time. Part of our difficulty is the constant lag between social structures and changing technology. The contraceptive pill changed the sexual, social and economic relationships between men and women. It enabled a new cultural dynamic of rapid change to be established that itself allowed the acceptance into the workplace of new technologies and practices that led to women increasingly becoming the majority of workers. Some want to reverse this and they argue that women should, in effect, return to the hearth. Crude popularizers traduce the fashionable vogue for evolutionary psychology by invoking support for the notion of fundamental gender differences in regard to work and home.

Another strand of the argument is to call upon employers to recognize that a happy worker is a better worker and that employees should be allowed to strike a better balance between home and work. This becomes entwined with the whole stakeholder idea and notions of corporate responsibility. While it is probably true that employees working in organizations with enlightened employment practices will feel happier and valued and may be even be more productive than others, there is little evidence that in the harshly competitive world that goes hand in glove with consumer capitalism, long-term success comes from being nice. Success comes not only from products and practices but also from knowing how to ride the economic cycles and increasingly how to allocate resources between countries. No multinational company would think twice about moving factories and offices if it made sense in what these firms call the 'bigger picture'. The organization has its own self-interest based on survival and that means that even well-intentioned and well-developed employee programmes are seldom embedded in the entrails of an organization.

The introduction of an always-open society will undoubtedly relieve some of the time pressures on people. It does mean shift work for all as one person's opportunity to shop late on a Saturday requires another to be working at that time. But this structural change offers a way out of the dilemma. It will create its own pressures because people will have to rethink the relationship between home, work and leisure if they are to make the new-found flexibility work to their benefit. There will be a need to find new ways of co-ordinating social activities. Individuals will not automatically share common hours for joint social and leisure activity. Likewise, the family will need to take more care in planning its joint events. Instead of maintaining itself simply through the daily routine, it will have to work harder to maintain itself as a cohesive unit.

The 24 Hour Society

The 24 Hour Society is mainly regarded in terms of shop opening hours. But it is far more than that. Eventually, it will lead to a different construction of daily activities, freeing people from the restraints and deadlines imposed at present by the rigid adherence to the clock. We will break away from the thinking that there are a fixed number of hours per day for selected activities and move into a more flexible and free-wheeling approach, co-ordinating activities on the fly.

There is a strong link between work hours, shopping and service hours, and transport. These in turn strongly affect patterns of land use. Government policies aimed at integrating transport or restricting land use need to include aspects of time. For example, smoothing out the working day over a longer period will reduce the present early morning and evening travel and congestion peaks, if not total travel. At present, transport systems have to cope with peak capacity for only four to six hours a day. They would operate more efficiently if there was more equal loading through the day and night. This might provide a solution to the current problem of ever more cars and congestion in a cost-effective way without having to introduce unpopular and punitive car-restrictions. Similarly, demand for all utilities and services will be smoothed out, reducing the inefficiencies produced by the need to have the capacity to meet the peak loads.

There is something inherently wrong in houses being empty half the time while people are at work, and workplaces being empty half the time while people are at home. If the working day was staggered over sixteen to eighteen hours, then offices, shops and schools would have at least double the usage they do now. If a shopping centre is open for twelve hours, the site would be more intensively used if a leisure element extended usage for a further four to five hours. In effect, we could get the same results as we do now from half the buildings, which would have a substantial impact on land-use policy.

There are some who would go much further than the 24 Hour Society and completely rethink the use of time. One Internet newsgroup suggestion is that we should switch to 28 hour days. Monday would be eliminated, on the basis that everyone hates Mondays. The work week would be four ten-hour shifts with a fifty-six-hour weekend. Thursday might be a problem, being dark most of the day, but as the originator of the idea has suggested, Thursdays could be used for roadworks.

The 24 Hour Society is not an automatic panacea to our time problems. It requires thoughtful participation if it is to help in redefining temporal relationships. But most important of all, it enables us to have a more egalitarian society in terms of who works when, frees us from the vicissitudes of living under clock time without losing the economic benefits, and provides a prospect of cities in the twenty-first century in which people can work, relax and play.

Notes

Introduction

1 BT/First Direct, *24 Hour Society Report*, Future Foundation 1998

2 Gary Cross, *Time and Money*, Routledge 1993

3 Murray Melbin, *Night as Frontier*, The Free Press 1987

Chapter 1

1 Quoted in Murray Melbin, *Night as Frontier*, The Free Press 1987

2 National Grid, private communication

3 BT, private communication

4 National Travel Survey (NTS), Office of National Statistics (ONS), 1996

5 Professor C. Cooper, *Daily Mail*, 5 March 1998

6 Robert Levine, *A Geography of Time*, Basic Books 1997

7 BT/First Direct survey, Future Foundation/NTS, 1998

Chapter 2

1 *Labour Market Trends*, ONS March 1998

2 TUC/MORI, *The Time of Our Lives*, 1998

3 Jonathan Gershuny, *ESRC: Perspectives on Work in the 1990s*, ESRC, August 1997

4 Arnie Rincover, *HealthCareer Web*, 1997

5 Trades Union Congress, *City-time Policies*, April 1998

6 Gallup, *Daily Telegraph*, 3 June 1996

7 *Social Trends*, HMSO 1995

8 Robert Caro, *The Years of Lyndon Johnson: Paths to Power*, Collins 1983

9 Christine Hardyment, *From Mangle to Microwave*, Polity Press 1988

10 American Demographics, March 1997

11 Quoted in Christine Hardyment, *From Mangle to Microwave*, Polity Press 1988

12 Oliver James, *Britain on the Couch: Why We're Unhappier Compared with 1950, Despite Being Richer*, Century 1997

13 BT/First Direct survey, Future Foundation/NTS 1998

14 IMS Global Services, reported on Infobeat, April 1998

15 Future Foundation/Channel 4, 1997

16 Juliet Schor, *The Overworked American: The Unexpected Decline of Leisure*, Basic Books 1993

17 Jack D. Schwager, *Market Wizards*, New York Institute of Finance (NYIF) 1989

18 Leon Kreitzman, *Encyclopaedia of Occupational Health and Safety*, International Labour Office, 1997

19 Institute of Management, *Are Managers Under Stress?*, September 1996

20 Klaus Vater, *The Conflict Over Working Hours*, Internationes 1980

21 Gary Cross, *Time and Money*, Routledge 1993

22 TUC, *The Time of our Lives*, TUC 1998

23 Shirley Conran, *Superwoman: Everywoman's Book of Household Management*, Sidgwick & Jackson 1975

24 Jeff Madrick, *New York Review of Books*, 26 March 1998

25 Fred van Raaij, *Journal of Economic Psychology* 1993, 14: 541

26 C. Usher, *Guardian*, 29 September 1998

27 Mastering Marketing 2, *Financial Times*, September 1998

Chapter 3

1 Jeremy Rifkin, *The End of Work*, Putnam, 1995

2 International Labour Organization, *World Employment Report*, ILO 1997/98

3 J. Madeau, Dade County Library Association Annual Workshop, 14 March 1997

4 *Labour Market Trends*, ONS, May 1998

5 David Brown, *Cybertrends*, Viking 1997

6 Anthony Giddens, *The Consequences of Modernity*, Polity Press 1990

7 World Travel and Tourism Council, 1995

8 Gerhard Dohrn van Rossum, *History of the Hour*, University of Chicago Press 1996

9 H. Leichter, *Free to be Foolish*, Princeton University Press 1991

Chapter 4

1 Alfred Marshall, *Principles of Economics III, II, I*, Macmillan 1948
2 Richard Dawkins, *The Selfish Gene*, Oxford University Press 1989
3 Robert Bocock, *Key Ideas in Consumption*, Routledge 1993
4 Colin Campbell, Romanticism and the consumer ethic, *Sociological Analysis* 1983, 44(4)
5 *Evening Standard*, 28 January 1998
6 Joshua Gordon Lippincott, *Design for Business*, P. Theobald 1947
7 Advertisement for Magic Holidays seen on London Underground, January 1998
8 Grant McCracken, *Culture and Consumption*, Indiana University Press 1988
9 Neil McKendrick, John Brewer and J.H. Plumb, *The Birth of a Consumer Society*, Europa 1982
10 George Rudé, *Paris and London in the 18th Century*, Fontana 1970
11 Henry Ford, quoted in J.-M. Dru, *Disruption: Overturning Conventions and Shaking Up the Marketplace*, Adweek 1996
12 Richard Barnet and John Cavanagh, *Global Dreams*, Simon & Schuster, 1994
13 Christopher Lasch, *The Culture of Narcissism*, Norton 1979
14 Ibid.
15 Cited in Gary Cross, *Time and Money*, Routledge 1993
16 Quoted in Stuart Ewen, *All Consuming Images*, Basic Books 1988
17 Peter Lunt and Sonia Livingstone, *Mass Consumption and Personal Identity*, Open University 1992
18 A.H. Halsey (ed.), *British Social Trends Since 1900*, Macmillan 1988
19 Peter Corrigan, *The Sociology of Consumption*, Sage 1997
20 Fred van Raaij, *Journal of Economic Psychology*, 1993, 14: 541–63
21 Celia Lury, *Consumer Culture*, Polity Press 1996
22 Fred van Raaij, *Journal of Economic Psychology*, 1993, 14: 541–63
23 Bart Kosko, *Fuzzy Thinking*, Flamingo 1993
24 Stanley Davis, *Futures Perfect*, Addison-Wesley 1987

Chapter 5

1 *New Scientist*, 1 November 1997

2   Barbara Adam, *Time Watch*, Polity Press 1995
3   Stephen Hawking, *A Brief History of Time: From the Big Bang to Black Holes*, Bantam 1988
4   Robert Levine, *A Geography of Time*, Basic Books 1997
5   E.P. Thompson, *Past and Present* 1967, 38
6   Robert Levine, *A Geography of Time*, Basic Books 1997
7   Edward T. Hall, *The Dance of Life: The Other Dimension of Time*, Anchor Press/Doubleday 1983
8   Ibid.
9   G.J. Whitrow, *Time in History*, Oxford University Press 1989
10 Lewis Mumford, *Technics and Civilisation*, Routledge & Kegan Paul 1934
11 D. Landes, *The Wealth and Poverty of Nations*, Little, Brown 1998
12 Thessalonians 3:10, 'If any would not work, neither should he eat' refers to work not in the sense of a job but simply as doing something useful
13 E.P. Thompson, *Time, Work-discipline and Industrial Capitalism*, Pluto 1967
14 Jeremy Rifkin, *Time Wars: The Primary Conflict in Human History*, Holt 1987
15 Barbara Adam, *Time and Social Theory*, Polity Press 1990
16 M. Castells, *The Rise of the Network Society*, Blackwell 1996
17 F. Cairncross, *The Death of Distance*, Orion 1997
18 G. Lipsitz, *Time Passages*, University of Minnesota 1990
19 C. Murphy, *Atlantic Magazine*, November 1996
20 D. Landes, *The Wealth and Poverty of Nations*, Little, Brown 1998
21 Bart Kosko, *Fuzzy Thinking*, Flamingo 1994
22 Ibid.
23 Aristotle, *De Interpretatione*, fourth century BC
24 The Buddha, *Majjhima-Nikaya*, sixth century BC
25 Robert Levine, *A Geography of Time*, Basic Books 1997
26 C. Usher, *Guardian*, 29 September 1998

Chapter 6

1   *Independent*, 22 July 1998
2   *Fortune*, July 1998
3   Robert Levine, *A Geography of Time*, Basic Books 1997

4   TUC, *Polls Apart*, April 1998
5   Losing control, *Management Today*, June 1998
6   *Guardian*, 23 October 1998
7   New Ways to Work, *Balanced Lives*, September 1995

Chapter 7

1   'Aristides', *The American Scholar*, summer 1995
2   Roger Gosden, *Cheating Time*, Macmillan 1996
3   Walter J. Schwartz, *The Scientist* 1995, 9 (11 December)
4   Arthur Winfree, quoted in Peter Coveney and Roger Highfield, *The Arrow of Time*, Flamingo 1991
5   George C. Williams, *Plan and Purpose in Nature*, Weidenfeld & Nicolson 1996
6   *Journal of the American Medical Association* 1996, 275: 1, 143–4.
7   Mayo Clinic, Mayo Clinic web-site (http://www.mayo.edu) 1998
8   *American Medical News*, 26 March 1996
9   David Dinges, *USA Today*, 19 April 1998
10 Michael Moore-Ede, *The Twenty Four Hour Society*, Addison-Wesley 1993
11 Peter Coveney and Roger Highfield, *The Arrow of Time*, Flamingo 1991
12 Stanley Coren, *The Sleep Thieves*, The Free Press 1996
13 Michael Young, *The Metronomic Society*, Thames & Hudson 1988
14 Ibid.
15 Stanley Coren, *The Sleep Thieves*, The Free Press 1996
16 Daniel Dennett, *Darwin's Dangerous Idea*, Penguin 1995
17 Carol Everson (University of Tennessee), *Scientific American*, July 1996
18 James Kreuger (University of Tennessee), *Scientific American*, July 1996
19 Ibid.
20 National Sleep Foundation, *Sleeplessness, Pain and the Workplace*, National Sleep Foundation 1995
21 Ibid.
22 Dr Michael Bonnet and Dr Donna Arend, *Electronic Telegraph*, 24 January 1996
23 Professor Jim Horne and Dr Yvonne Harrison, Loughborough University

24 Professor Jim Horne, Loughborough University

25 Stephen Mennell, *Norbert Elias*, Blackwell 1992

26 Ibid.

27 *Evening Standard*, 13 May 1998

28 Richard Coleman, *The 24-Hour Business*, Amacom 1995

29 A.B. Dollins, R. Wurtman *et al.*, *Proceedings of the National Academy of Sciences of the United States of America* 1994, 91

30 Rae Silver (Columbia University, New York), *Scientific American*, April 1998

31 *Sunday Times*, 14 June 1998

32 Rockefeller University press release, 25 March 1996

33 J. Takahashi *et al.*, *Science*, 23 May 1997

Chapter 8

1   Karl Marx, *Das Kapital*, vol. 1 chapter X, International Publishers 1933

2   Simon Folkard, *The Scotsman*, 4 March 1998

3   Royal College of Nursing, *Taking Part Survey*, RCN September 1997

4   H. Prosser, Jobs, Family and Gender, *Demography*, November 1995

5   Richard Coleman, *The 24-Hour Business*, Amacom 1995

6   Simon Folkard (Swansea University), 24 Hour Society conference, London, February 1998

7   Martin Moore-Ede, *The Twenty Four Hour Society*, Addison-Wesley 1993

8   Dr Russell Foster (Imperial College, London), 24 Hour Society conference, London, February 1998

9   BT/First Direct, *24 Hour Consumer Survey*, BT/First Direct 1997

10 Stanley Coren, *The Sleep Thieves*, The Free Press 1996

11 *Sunday Times* (Scotland), 1 March 1998

12 T. Scitovsky, *The Joyless Economy*, Oxford University Press 1992

13 D.C. Whitehead, H. Thomas and D.R. Slapper, 'A rational approach to shift-work in emergency medicine', *Medicine* 1992, 21: 1250–8

14 Richard Coleman, *The 24-Hour Business*

Chapter 9

1   Alvin Toffler, *Powershift*, Bantam 1990

2   *Guardian*, 29 October 1997

3   Stanley Davis, *Future Perfect*, Addison-Wesley 1987

4   *Financial Times*, 29 August 1998

5   Dan Dimancescu, Peter Hines and Nick Rich, *The Lean Enterprise*, Amacom 1997

6   BT/First Direct survey, Future Foundation/NTS 1998

Chapter 10

1   Jonathan Miller, *Emerging Trends in Real Estate*, Equitable Insurance 1997

2   Fourth 24 Hour City conference, Sheffield, 1996

3   Birmingham City Council, *City Living Progress Report*, 1997

4   Rosemary Betterton, Fourth 24 Hour City Conference, Sheffield 1996

5   Ibid.

6   J. Montgomery, *The Evening Economy of Cities* (Conference on Nighttime Economy), Manchester Institute of Popular Culture 1994

7   Bolton Town Centre Partnership, *For a Night in the Town*, 1998

8   Richard Rogers, *Cities For a Small Planet*, Faber & Faber 1997

9   Ibid.

10 Jane Jacobs, *Death and Life of Great American Cities*, Cape 1961

11 Andrew Marr, *Observer*, 12 July 1998

12 Roy Ascott, *Times Higher Education*, 16 September 1994

13 Jonathan Miller, *Emerging Trends in Real Estate*, Equitable Insurance 1997

14 Andy Lovatt, *Towards the 24 Hour City?*, Manchester Institute of Popular Culture, 1994

Chapter 11

1   Quentin Letts, *Evening Standard*, 26 September 1997

2   Jean Chesneaux, *Brave Modern World*, Thames & Hudson 1992

3   Juliet Schor, Doors of Perception conference, 1996

4   Herodotus, *Histories*, book 2, chapter 133, fifth century BC

5   A. Gummere, *The Quaker*, New York 1968

Bibliography

World Employment Report, Geneva, ILO, 1998.

24 Hour Society, London, NTS/Future Foundation, 1998.

Time of Our Lives, London, TUC, 1998.

Social Trends, London, Office of National Statistics, 1995.

Adam B., *Time Watch*, Oxford, Polity Press, 1995.

Adam B., *Time and Social Theory*, Oxford, Polity Press, 1990.

Barnet R. and Cavanagh J., *Global Dreams*, New York, Simon & Schuster, 1994.

Bocock R., *Key Ideas in Consumption*, London, Routledge, 1993.

Brown D., *Cybertrends*, London, Viking, 1997.

Cairncross F., *The Death of Distance*, London, Orion, 1997.

Caro R., *The Years of Lyndon Johnson*, Collins, 1983.

Castells M., *The Rise of the Network Society*, Oxford, Blackwell, 1996.

Chesneaux J., *Brave Modern World*, London, Thames & Hudson, 1992.

Coleman R., *The 24-Hour Business*, New York, Amacom, 1995.

Conran S., *Superwoman: Everywoman's Book of Household Management*, London, Sidgwick & Jackson, 1975.

Coren S., *The Sleep Thieves*, New York, The Free Press, 1996.

Corrigan P., *The Sociology of Consumption*, London, Sage, 1997.

Coveney P. and Highfield R., *The Arrow of Time*, London, Flamingo, 1991.

Cross G., *Time and Money*, London, Routledge, 1993.

Csikszentmihalyi M., *Flow*, London, Rider, 1998.

Davis S., *Futures Perfect*, New York, Addison-Wesley, 1987.

Dawkins R., *The Selfish Gene*, Oxford, Oxford University Press, 1989.

Dennett D., *Darwin's Dangerous Idea*, London, Penguin, 1995.

Dimancescu D., Hines P. and Rich N., *The Lean Enterprise*, New York, Amacom, 1997.

Dohrn-van Rossum G., *History of the Hour*, Chicago, University of Chicago Press, 1996.

Dru J. M., *Disruption: Overturning Conventions and Shaking Up the Marketplace*, New York, Adweek, 1996.

Ewen S., *All Consuming Images*, New York, Basic Books, 1988.

Gershuny J., *Perspectives on work in the 1990s*, Colchester, ESRC, 1997.

Giddens A., *The Consequences of Modernity*, London, Polity Press, 1990.

Gosden J., *Cheating Time*, London, Macmillan, 1996.

Gunmere A., *The Quaker*, New York, 1968.

Hall E. T., *The Dance of Life*, New York, Doubleday, 1983.

Halsey A. H., *British Social Trends since 1900*, London, Macmillan, 1988.

Hardyment C., *From Mangle to Microwave*, London, Polity Press, 1988.

Hawking S., *A Brief History of Time: From the Big Bang to Black Holes*,
    New York, Bantam, 1988.

Jacobs J., *Death and Life of Great American Cities*, New York, Cape, 1961.

James O., *Britain on the Couch*, London, Century, 1997.

Kosko B., *Fuzzy Thinking*, London, Flamingo, 1993.

Kreitzman L., *ILO Encyclopaedia of Occupational Health*, Geneva, ILO,
    1997.

Landes D., *The Wealth and Poverty of Nations*, London, Little, Brown, 1998.

Lasch C., *The Culture of Narcissism*, New York, Norton, 1979.

Lebergott S., *Pursuing Happiness*, Princeton, Princeton University Press,
    1993.

Leichter, *Free to be Foolish*, Princeton, Princeton University Press, 1991.

Levine R., *A Geography of Time*, New York, Basic Books, 1997.

Lippincott J. G., *Design for Business*, Chicago, 1947.

Lipsitz G., *Time Passages*, Minneapolis, University of Minnesota Press, 1990.

Lovatt A., *Towards the 24 Hour City*, Manchester, Institute of Popular
    Culture, 1994.

Lunt P. and Livingstone S., *Mass Consumption and Personal Identity*, Milton
    Keynes, Open University Press, 1992.

Lury C., *Consumer Culture*, London, Polity Press, 1996.

Marshall A., *Principles of Economics*, Macmillan, 1948.

Marx K., *Das Kapital*, International Publishers, 1933.

McCracken G., *Culture and Consumption*, Indiana University Press, 1988.

McKendrick N., Brewer J. and Plumb J. H., *The Birth of Consumer Society*,
    London, Europa, 1982.

Melbin M., *Night as Frontier*, New York, The Free Press, 1987.

Mennell S., *Norbert Elias*, Oxford, Blackwell, 1992.

Miller J., *Emerging Trends in Real Estate*, New York, Equitable Insurance, 1997.

Montgomery J., *The Evening Economy of Cities*, Manchester, Institute of Popular Culture, 1994.

Moore-Ede M., *The Twenty Four Hour Society*, Menlo Park, Addison-Wesley, 1993.

Mumford L., *Technics and Civilisation*, London, Routledge and Kegan Paul, 1934.

Rifkin J., *The End of Work*, New York, Putnams, 1995.

Rifkin J., *Time Wars*, New York, Henry Holt, 1987.

Rogers R., *Cities For a Small Planet*, London, Faber & Faber, 1997.

Rudé G., *Paris and London in the 18th Century*, London, Fontana, 1970.

Schor J., *The Overworked American*, New York, Basic Books, 1993.

Schwager J., *Market Wizards*, New York, New York Institute of Finance, 1989.

Scitovsky T., *The Joyless Economy*, Oxford, Oxford University Press, 1992.

Thompson E. P., 'Time, Work-Discipline and Industrial Capitalism', *Past and Present*, 38, 1967.

Toffler A., *Powershift*, New York, Bantam, 1990.

Vater K., *The Conflict Over Working Hours*, Internationes, 1980.

Whitrow G. J., *Time in History*, Oxford, Oxford University Press, 1989.

Young M., *The Metronomic Society*, London, Thames & Hudson, 1988.

Index